Joan Koob Cannie is chairwoman and founder of Learning Dynamics, Inc., one of the industry's leaders in developing and delivering human behavior skill training for professional and personal development.

Joan has been an entrepreneur since age 24. At that time she started her own New York advertising agency, Joan M. Koob Associates, which she operated successfully for fifteen years. She is also co-founder of the Investment Management Trust of Boston, and author of numerous articles and books, seasoned public speaker, and workshop facilitator for industry and government agencies (see *Who's Who in American Women*). She knows the special problems of women in the male-dominated world of the achieving organization, and has trained hundreds of women to deal effectively with these problems.

She's feminine, tough, and a believer in dealing with male chauvinism with grace and humor—rather than aggression. When a man tells her "You think just like a man," her favorite response is "A dumb one or a bright one?"

The Woman's Guide to Management Success

How to Win Power in the Real Organizational World

JOAN KOOB CANNIE

A SPECTRUM BOOK

PRENTICE-HALL, INC., *Englewood Cliffs, New Jersey 07632*

Library of Congress Cataloging in Publication Data

CANNIE, JOAN KOOB.
    The woman's guide to management success.

    (Spectrum books)
    Includes bibliographical references and index.
    1. Management.   2. Women executives.   I. Title.
HD38.C335   658.4'002'4042   78-31936
ISBN 0–13–961771–X
ISBN 0–13–961763–9 pbk.

Editorial/production supervision
and interior design by Claudia Citarella
Cover design by Ben Kann
Manufacturing buyer: Cathie Lenard

A SPECTRUM BOOK

Printed in the United States of America

10   9   8   7   6   5   4   3   2   1

PRENTICE-HALL INTERNATIONAL, INC., *London*

PRENTICE-HALL OF AUSTRALIA PTY. LIMITED, *Sydney*

PRENTICE-HALL OF CANADA, LTD., *Toronto*

PRENTICE-HALL OF INDIA PRIVATE LIMITED, *New Delhi*

PRENTICE-HALL OF JAPAN, INC., *Tokyo*

PRENTICE-HALL OF SOUTHEAST ASIA PTE. LTD., *Singapore*

WHITEHALL BOOKS LIMITED, *Wellington, New Zealand*

Contents

Introduction   ix

1
Getting Comfortable Managing Others   1

SELF-CONCEPT, 3
THE SEARCH FOR HARMONY, 5
THE INFORMAL ORGANIZATIONAL CLIMATE, 9
THE DYNAMIC SYSTEM, 12
SUM-UP, 26

2
Women and Men Are Different . . . But the *Job* Is the Same   27

THE POSITIVES AND THE NEGATIVES OF BEING "TRAINED" AS A
FEMALE, 28
OVERCOMING THE NEGATIVES OF BEING TRAINED AS A WOMAN, 33
USING THE POSITIVES OF BEING TRAINED AS A WOMAN, 38
FUNCTIONS OF MANAGERS, 41
SUM-UP, 45

3

The High Achiever Leadership Style   46

YOUR LEADERSHIP STYLE, 47
CREATING THE BEST JOB CLIMATE MOTIVATION, 54
DIMENSIONS OF THE JOB CLIMATE, 57
SUM-UP, 70

4

What Makes People Tick   71

BASIC HUMAN NEEDS, 74
SELF-DEFEATING BEHAVIOR, 80
PERSONALITY NEEDS, 86
SUM-UP, 90

5

Barriers to Communication   92

BARRIERS TO COMMUNICATION, 94
SUM-UP, 106

6

Trust-Building Skills: Listening, Attending, Stroking, and Reflection   108

LISTENING, 109
ATTENDING: THE BASIC NONVERBAL SKILL, 111
STROKING: THE BASIC VERBAL SKILL, 113
REFLECTION, 118
SUM-UP, 130

7

Negotiating and Persuading   131

THE THREATENING QUESTION, 132
THE TENTATIVE PHASE, 143
CONTRACTING, 147
SUM-UP, 151

8

Conflicts   152

CONFLICTS AMONG YOUR WORKERS, 153
INTERPERSONAL CONFLICTS, 155
CONFLICTS RELATED TO BEING A WOMAN, 166
SUM-UP, 170

9

Management by Objectives   171

PROBLEMS WITH TRADITIONAL EVALUATION TECHNIQUES, 173
MBO: MAKING IT WORK, 173
MAKING ORGANIZATIONAL AND INDIVIDUAL GOALS MESH, 184
YOUR GOALS AND PRIORITIES, 185
EFFICIENCY VS. EFFECTIVENESS, 185
UPWARD APPRAISAL, 186
CAUTIONS ABOUT MBO, 188
SUM-UP, 188

10

Decision-Making   189

THE INFORMAL SYSTEM OF RELATIONSHIPS, 190
BUILDING RELATIONSHIPS, 194
MAKING DECISIONS, 201

11

Increasing Your Effectiveness   210

TIME, 211
ORGANIZING YOUR TIME, 212
OTHER WAYS TO INCREASE YOUR EFFECTIVENESS, 218

Index   225
Index   225

Introduction

Before you start this book, I want to tell you a little about myself because I want you to feel comfortable about me.

I'm a high school graduate; I started my first company when I was 25, and have started three others since then. In doing so, I've made nearly every mistake in the book, and dealt with most of the problems, including the discrimination, well-meaning putdowns, and sex exploitation by others. I've learned how to deal with my own ineffective behavior, too: shy or aggressive, acting in ways I thought were expected of me instead of being myself, being too emotional at the wrong times, and most of all, not doing my job well because I feared people would reject or disapprove of me. But slowly—ever so slowly—I've learned to succeed in what was pretty much a man's world . . . but it took me over twenty years.

I tell you this because I want you to know I've been there. I'm no ivory tower theorist; I can show you my scars. I have had as much "little ladies don't . . ." conditioning as most women—maybe more. So, no matter what *anyone* says, and no matter how anxious or insecure you may feel, I know that if I could do it through self-education, you can do it, too. And it won't take twenty years. With this book, you can learn the skills of managing others and then do the job better than most men.

As a woman, you have some key skills most men don't have. For example, because of your special training in learning to be "feminine," you're probably more empathetic, you listen better, and you're far more sensitive to feelings. These are powerful advantages in working effectively through other people. At the same time, you have learned some negative attitudes and behaviors that hurt you as a manager. So you need to unlearn these negatives and get comfortable in the organizational climate as it *really is*.

Very few women understand the organizational climate as it really is. They come into this climate with a different mind-set than men . . . and they behave differently, much to their everlasting disadvantage.

HOW DO WOMEN BEHAVE IN THIS CLIMATE?

Advertising agency executive:

I often tell white lies. It's hard to always tell the truth or say no. I don't like to hurt people's feelings. I make up excuses. Or I stay late and do a project myself rather than ask someone to do it over.

Assistant bank treasurer:

My professional life is full of opportunities I didn't get because I didn't ask for them. I've never managed a department myself. I have always been assistant manager. But I've been afraid if I spoke up, I'd be thought too aggressive.

Research consultant:

I react the opposite way. I let others know that nobody messes with me. I'm rough and tough and mean. I know it's defensive and born out of fear I'll look stupid or weak. But I don't seem to be able to stop.

Editor:

There are so many things I'm not good at. I'm shy. I'm awkward talking to top management. I'm totally incompetent in the informal business rituals—like small talk and tradeoffs in meetings. I get nervous and use twenty words when one will do, and I have the mouth of a truck driver. I've done alright because I'm a great laborer. I work three times harder than others . . . but I cry a lot.

Know anyone like these women? *You,* maybe, at some point in your career—or even now? Well, I've been all of these women at one point or another, and I can tell you what this behavior gets you. It gets you the small office with no view and no carpet on the floor . . . if you're lucky. It gets you asked to take the notes in a meeting. It gets you passed over for promotions. It wins you put-downs and cracks behind your back about women. And it buys you a lot of resentment, indifference, and not much loyalty or dedicated hard work from your subordinates.

Then, when people treat you badly, take advantage of you, and hurt you, you feel worse—either more worthless and insignificant, or nastier, depending on your style. And you are locked into a vicious, unhappy cycle that keeps you from growing and moving ahead.

The sad thing is that nobody does this *to* you. For the most part, you do it to yourself. Yes, all that seemingly innocent passive or aggressive behavior creates most of your problems. For example, most women take criticism personally. If an idea of theirs is criticized, they say "I'm stupid," rather than "the *idea* is bad." One skill you'll learn in this book is how to deal with criticism without getting defensive . . . or crying (which permits men to say, "Emotional women!").

Another example: most women wait to be asked. All their lives they've heard: "*Wait* to be invited on a date," "*Wait* to be asked to get married." But if you wait to be asked if you want a promotion, you will rarely get one; further, *you'll look as if you don't want one*. This is because, by waiting until you're asked, you don't seem motivated. In this book, you'll learn some new skills for speaking up, asking for promotions or advanced opportunities, competing with others, and taking risks.

Most women have little power within the organization—and don't know how to get more. In this book, you'll learn what power is, how to get it, and how to use it. You'll learn how to exercise the unique advantages you have because you are a woman—and these are advantages which help tune you in to the informal power structure—and get you what you want. Being a mouse *or* a bully will get you nowhere in most organizations. Neither will staying aloof or distant from the real world. You need to learn to play the game.

But this is all a matter of learning new skills—that is, new *behavior*. And if you work at these skills, the results will be your own personal growth . . . and your happiness and management success as well.

1
Getting
Comfortable
Managing Others

Human behavior science has amassed an incredible amount of data showing that the dominant factor in human achievement is behavior. Not intelligence, not education, not technical ability. Just behavior! Something we all do—the only difference being in how we do it.[1]

If you aspire to a management position or if you *are* a manager and want to go further up the ladder, I think this book will help you. It's purpose is to teach you new behavior, the kind of behavior that succeeds at the management level of most organizations.

Let's start by defining the term "manager." A manager is responsible for producing results, just like everyone else who works. But a manager's *method* of achieving results is different from a non-manager. A manager's results are achieved by others, not by him- or herself. And to achieve results through others, a manager needs special skills which others don't need. In other words, management is a profession in itself with it's own responsibilities and skills, that is, *behaviors*.

All of your behavior—including your actions, thoughts, feelings, body language, and emotions—is uniquely yours. And who controls your behavior? You do. Then who is really responsible for your success or failure in your career? You bet—*you* are. But even so, chances are that you need some help in learning positive new behavior and in throwing out unwanted, negative ways of behaving. So let's start there. How did you learn to be who you are and to behave the way you do? Let's see.

[1]From a recent study (Achieving Manager Research Project) by Teleometrics International, The Woodlands, Texas.

SELF-CONCEPT

Who are you? You are the center of the world. Yes, you live at the center of a private and constantly changing world . . . and so does everyone else. Think of this center as your self-concept, or the unique, one-of-a-kind you. It is the sum total of all you refer to when you think of "I" or "me." It is you from your own point of view.

Your self-concept was developed by four key influences:

1. Your physical self or your body image
2. The parental feedback and conditioning you received
3. Your experience with others and the world, which shaped your personality
4. Your values and your goals.

Let's take a closer look at these influences.

Body Self

Almost as soon as you were born, you began to develop your first view of yourself—your body self. As an infant, you began to identify your body when you felt discomfort, or when you felt good as your needs were satisfied. Soon, you began to see yourself as a person—a female—strong or weak, thin or fat, black, white, or another color; normal or handicapped; and so on.

This sense of body self was the beginning of your self-concept. And, although it is not your entire sense of self, it does remain, to some degree, a lifelong anchor for your self-concept. You can understand how important your sense of body self is by performing an imaginary experiment presented by Gordon Allport in his book, *Becoming: Basic Considerations for a Psychology of Personality*. He writes:

> Think first of swallowing the saliva in your mouth, or do so. Then, imagine expectorating it into a tumbler and drinking it! What seemed

natural and "mine" suddenly becomes disgusting and alien . . . in the twinkling of an eye.[2]

What you think of as belonging intimately to your body is warm and welcome; but what you think of as separate from your body can be cold and foreign—even repulsive.

Parental Feedback

As you grew older, your physical or body self came to influence the way you behaved. If you were reasonably normal, so too in all probability was your behavior. But another factor—which was enormously significant—began to affect you. You were a girl—not a boy. And this influenced the reactions and feedback you were getting from your parents and others who were close to you.

Most parents are more protective of girls than boys. And if, for example, they discouraged you from competition, games, and risk-taking, you may have decided you needed protection, and so you avoided competition and risks.

Or maybe you were strong and outgoing, and your mother disapproved of your behavior. She let you know your behavior was not acceptable to her, or to the world. This feedback may have encouraged you to behave passively—to conform with the world's view of you.

Almost all of us have been influenced by this type of parental feedback. And, although you may in time outgrow the specific patterns of childhood, your early experience with such feedback to your behavior is at the core of your self-concept.

Influence of Others

As you continued to grow and your field of perception widened, your daily experiences, your interaction with your world, and particularly the *judgment of you by others*, formed another aspect of your self-concept. You learned that girls are different from boys, do different things, behave in different ways. As a female, you learned a set of assumptions about the

[2]Gordon Allport, *Becoming: Basic Considerations for a Psychology of Personality* (New Haven,: Yale University Press, 1955), pp. 40–56.

way the world is and about how to behave in it. Specifically, if you are like most women, you were learning how to attract and win a husband. Your focus was on how you looked rather than on what you could or couldn't do to support yourself for the rest of your life. This, in turn, affected all of your personal qualities: coldness or warmth, weakness or toughness, humor or lack of it, and so on—the YOU that is uniquely you. In a word, your personality.

Values and Goals

As your personality was developing, you were also evolving a system of values by which you could operate. These values, these personal rules, were shaped by your own experience and by the judgment of your behavior by others. Sometimes this judgment of your behavior may have caused you to simply take your values from others, without having had any direct experience of your own. But, regardless of how you arrived at them, you developed a set of values or irreducible positions beyond which you will not go. And these values, in turn, have helped you shape your goals.

For example, you may place such a high value on your family life that you would refuse a job that would greatly reduce the time you could spend with your family, even though it pays more than you are now making. You may value working alone more than you do competing with others. You may value security more than taking risks. Or you may not even have any clear values about a career. Will you or won't you? If so, for how long?

THE SEARCH FOR HARMONY

Of course, the number of ways you may see yourself is practically limitless, but your self-concept is the organization of all of these views into a single system. And it is this system that you feel compelled to defend.

You live at the center of this system, and you are striving constantly to keep the outside world in tune with your world. The problem is that the environment of the management world is, as we shall see, in direct conflict with your learned behavior. So you are, in effect, a battlefield—striving for harmony between your self-concept and pressures from a world you don't really understand.

Let's go back for a moment to a point made earlier. *An important part of your self-concept and your values is determined by the judgments of your behavior by others.*

Early Training

Stop now for a moment and think how you spent the first twenty-odd years of your life. What were you doing? What was happening to you? If you are like most women, you were being trained by parents and educated by teachers. Although they probably meant well, these people who had so much influence on your self-concept spent much of the time during your first twenty years correcting you by judging your behavior, and by training you to be dependent and passive. Can you remember the types of things you grew up hearing? Before you were in your teens, you might have heard: "What a good girl—you didn't spill," or "Little ladies don't behave that way," or "What a little love—you brought Daddy his paper."

Then, as you grew older, you might have heard things like: "Young ladies don't boast about good marks," or "She doesn't seem quite the right friend for you, dear," or "I know your younger brother stays out until 11:00, but he's a boy."

Later on: "When are you going to do something about your hair and complexion? You'll never catch a man if you don't take care of yourself."

As a result, you learned you were different from boys—more limited in what you could do in life. And now, like most of us, you probably have made a great many decisions about yourself, like "I'm shy," "I'm nervous," "I'm a loner," "I'm afraid to take risks," "I'm sensitive," "I'm emotional," "I'm helpless." The problem with these negative decisions is first that they chain you to the past and keep you from growing as a human being; and second that they keep you from developing the kind of behavior you need as a manager.

Most women lived through this kind of "little ladies" training, and it has built into us a sense of dependency, inadequacy, inflexibility, noncompetitiveness, and the like.

We may not think of ourselves as equal to men, or we may suppress behavior we think isn't "feminine." This makes many of us feel weak and not too bright, and gives us a sense of self-disapproval that is so automatic it is hard to recognize. And it makes us too sensitive to criticism, and often too emotional. But there is more to it than this low opinion many of us have of ourselves.

Learning Phony Roles

Most women have not been conditioned for the team play that is essential in operating effectively in the informal organizational structure. Almost all boys learn early in life that you need to have eleven for a football team. And with this training, they learn about competition, cooperation, taking criticism, winning, and losing. Thus, men have had a lifelong conditioning to be flexible, make plans, have alternative plans, take risks, and most importantly in the organizational power network, how to make tradeoffs and deals. Most women don't learn these things, and so they are at a distinct disadvantage when they step into management.

Here's an extreme example of how women become handicapped by their upbringing as females. The words are those of a remarkable Canadian woman attending one of my seminars:

> I was born of poor farmers. My mother was Indian and my father a remote, strict authoritarian. I loved working outdoors but it was forbidden because that's what my brother did. I worked in the house. I got good grades in school and wanted to go on, but all I ever heard was, "You're a woman. You don't need an education. Besides, you're part Indian, so you'll never get anywhere or be anything. There's no point in even trying."

> I had a grandmother who saved me—my father's mother. She encouraged me, praised me, kept my hope alive. My mother detested her and did everything she could to prevent me from being "contaminated" by her. At 18, I joined the Armed Forces and escaped. But to this day, I'm scared of anything new. I was a doormat to my husband, and a perfect slave to all my previous bosses. And although I've been a successful model, I still never saw myself as attractive— just a worthless, dumb, part Indian.

Of course, this kind of behavior is crippling. We see ourselves in a certain way. That's reality to us. So naturally, we behave according to this view. But what if our view of reality is wrong, or if the reality of our environment is in conflict with our *view* of reality? Then, sadly, we live a phony role. And in doing so, we create *more* problems for ourselves.

Evaluating Your Roles

What about you? What phony roles are you aware of playing? Good assistant? Tough broad? Clinging vine? Poor little thing? One way to find out is to do the Who Am I exercise.

Exercise

On a sheet of paper answer the question "Who am I?" nine times by writing a description of yourself and your roles. Then rank them in their order of importance from 1 through 9. (Number 1 is the most important.) Now examine your list and separate your roles (what you do) from your identity (who you are). Then ask: Are these roles real, or are they my way of defending my self-concept?

Evaluating Your Goals

Let's discuss ways of getting rid of phony roles. A role depends on the goals you have set, or those your parents set for you. So one good way to eliminate phony roles is to re-evaluate your existing goals and change them if necessary.

Exercise

Answer these questions: What are my goals in various areas of my life? Where do I want to be two years from now, five years from now, ten years from now? What is the highest position I hope to attain? How much money would satisfy me? How much free time do I want? Do I want a career? For how long? What do I honestly want to be, gain, or do in life?

Next, list your interests, skills, talents, aptitudes, likes, dislikes, and limitations. Then examine what you have written. Are your goals compatible with the interests, skills, abilities, strengths, and weaknesses you listed? Now answer the questions: Are my goals realistic? Are they in line with my talents? Am I aiming too high? Or am I not aiming high enough?

If the goals aren't realistic, or if you're aiming too low or too high under your present circumstances, go back and rewrite your goals.

One of the biggest problems for women is that they make their career decision late—perhaps ten years after they have started working. This puts them at a great disadvantage. Superiors don't see them as serious about a career, or motivated. Many women act as helpers or followers, not *doers*. Or they carve out a little world of their own in which they become indispensable. And all of this works to their disadvantage when the time for promotion arrives. How about you? Have you really made a career commitment? To find out, take the Career Commitment Quiz (see Table 1.1).

THE INFORMAL
ORGANIZATIONAL CLIMATE

Now let's take a look at the informal organizational climate—what it's really like and what it takes to succeed in it.

Dr. Gene Booker illustrates the informal world of organizations by presenting an image where different lengths of yarn are strung from the ceiling to the floor and to the four walls, until an entire room is filled with intersecting and connecting lines. These pieces of yarn represent power influence and interpersonal impacts to complicate it even further, some of these pieces of yarn are of different lengths and some have offshoots; others have weights attached to them. Still further, every other month or so various weights on the different lines change; new lines go up, and old ones are removed.

TABLE 1.1
Career Commitment Quiz

Have You Made a Career Commitment?

People who are not committed to a career usually don't get promoted. Have you made that commitment yet? To find out, circle the answer that is closest to the way you feel.

1. I plan to work
   a. the rest of my life.
   b. until age 65.
   c. a few more years.

   d. until I marry or have children.

2. I would most like to be
   a. company president.

TABLE 1.1 (Continued)

b. senior executive.

c. middle manager.

d. supervisor.

3. I would like to earn
   a. $100,000 or more a year.
   b. $50,000.
   c. $25,000.
   d. $12,500.

4. I am willing to work
   a. 10 or more hours a day.
   b. 8–9 hours a day.
   c. 7½–8 hours a day.
   d. 7 or fewer hours a day.

5. If I were offered a special project due in one week, involving 20 hours' extra work, I would
   a. work nights and weekends to finish it as soon as possible.
   b. work an extra 3 hours a day for one week.
   c. ask to be relieved of other work to do the project.
   d. refuse the project.

6. If I had a baby, I would
   a. leave work only long enough to bear the child.
   b. leave work until it was old enough for day care.
   c. quit work until it entered elementary school.
   d. quit work at least until all my children left home.

7. I feel my husband or best male friend's job is
   a. less important than mine.
   b. about the same as mine in importance.
   c. somewhat more important than mine.
   d. a lot more important than mine.

8. If my husband were offered a significantly better job in another state, I would
   a. refuse to move.
   b. refuse to move until I located a comparable job.
   c. begin looking immediately for another job.
   d. stop working since we no longer would need the money.

Scoring:

3 for each "a" answer	*1 for each "c" answer*
2 for each "b" answer	*0 for each "d" answer*

Interpretation:

19–24: You seem totally committed to a management career.

13–18: You seem to definitely want a management career, but that is not your top priority.

7–12: You seem unsure whether you want a career.

0–6: You do not seem to want a career.

Reprinted by courtesy of Learning Dynamics, Inc., from the "Professional Woman Manager" program, Session I, 1977.

This complicated set of interrelationships illustrates that your work as a manager is directly tied to the influence and power of others. And this power and influence change all the time.

Silber and Sherman describe it this way in *Managerial Performance and Promotability*:[3]

> The informal world of organization life is one of influence, power, flexible tradeoffs, and negotiation. If you think for one minute that your ideas get through the system because they are right, they are the best, they are the only way to fly, then you are living in a fantasy world. Things happen in any organizational structure because of negotiations, tradeoffs, selling, and a continuing succession of informal coalitions.
>
> Being aware of the informal world is being aware of the changing sub rosa relationships, the person-to-person sensitivities, the informal political values and taboos, and the informal understandings between functions and among people within the functions as well as knowing what thou shalt and shalt not do. Arrangements within this unstructured world are seldom written down; there are no descriptions of the informal interpersonal credit bank—in fact, the entire power dimension is never fully described. You must gain your awareness by tuning in to the arrangement to sense who has the clout, power, influence, direction.

Many people, women in particular, find it difficult to live in this informal world. They like to have things spelled out neatly. They believe that if you want to get something done, you must go through the system, rigidly following its procedures and practices. But that's not the way it is. The undeniable reality is that people in management live in a world in which the relationships of power and influence are constantly changing.

If you are tuned in to this world, you know who was in power last month. You are aware of who has the contacts, who is the power behind the throne, who is the person to see to get something done. You also know who has fallen from favor and is no longer influential. In fact, knowing who is in and who can make things happen is basic to success in the informal world.

Some women are not progressing in their careers and don't know why. They can't understand why they are ineffective, because they have done everything according to the book. Yet the book is not everything. If

[3]Mark B. Silber and V. Clayton Sherman, *Managerial Performance and Promotability: The Making of an Executive* (New York: American Management Assn., Inc., 1974), pp. 5–6.

you are blind to this dynamic environment, then it will catch you short, punish you, and eventually decrease your effectiveness. Some women have difficulty living with the ambiguity and the anxiety that it creates; others cannot live with it at all. They are unable to deal with the intrigue and the importance of keeping their senses tuned in to who is in power and how things are done in the organization world.

Of course, as we have seen, there are good reasons why most women don't understand or know how to operate in this climate. Yet, to succeed, you need to learn how—or else make the decision that life in a large-scale organization is not for you.

Figure 1.1 will help you understand the dynamic informal organization better.

THE DYNAMIC SYSTEM

This is a simplified view of a dynamic system. The Dynamic Systems Theory is the work of the eminent scientist, Ludwig von Bertalanffy—and it is turning the world of human behavior upside down, because it represents a totally new way of understanding yourself, your environment, and your relationships with others.[4]

The system is made up of three parts: (1) input, (2) reality, and (3) feedback.

Seeing yourself and your environment as a system will give you one of the most important tools in life for your personal growth. This is true because *any change* in your input can change the feedback. And since you control the input, this gives you a tremendous degree of control over things.

Input, Reality, and Feedback

Let's look at input—the behavior of the average woman when she makes the transition into a management position. Because of her past "training" as a female in this world, most of her actions and reactions will

[4]Ludwig von Bertalanffy, *General System Theory* (New York: George Braziller, Inc., 1968), pp. 191–96.

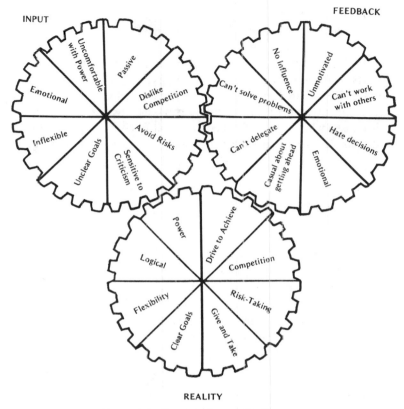

INPUT

FEEDBACK

REALITY

Figure 1.1 Dynamic Personality System

not be based on the reality of the *system*. As women, we are disadvantaged because

1. We are passive rather than assertive; i.e., we are followers and helpers rather than doers—and we don't speak up.
2. We dislike competition.
3. We avoid risks.
4. We're sensitive to criticism.
5. Our goals are usually unclear.
6. We are not very flexible—we want to "do our own thing."

Figure 1.1 reprinted by courtesy of Learning Dynamics, Inc., from the "Professional Woman Manager" program, Session I, 1977.

7. We are emotional and express feelings.
8. We are uncomfortable exercising power.

We've seen that the reality of the job climate is influence, power, tradeoffs, competition, clear goals, flexibility, and risk taking.

Chances are that your input—the way you are likely to behave—is in direct conflict with the reality of the system—the organizational demands. In that case, what kind of feedback are you likely to produce? In other words, how are the people in your environment likely to see and behave toward you?

They will see you as

1. Not too motivated
2. Unable to work with others
3. Unable to make decisions
4. Oversensitive, overemotional
5. Too casual about getting ahead
6. A hard worker—but one who can't *lead*
7. Unable to anticipate problems or to solve them
8. A person with no influence

In short, your input into the system is producing negative feedback, which prevents you from rising in management.

If you are behaving in these ways—and most women are—what can you do?

Spelling Out Future Goals

You have already taken the first step; you've evaluated your goals. Now you need to spell out your future goals. Perhaps you have overinvested in a particular technical skill—one that is not a visible and transferable management skill. So next, you need to develop a plan that will get you from where you are to where you want to go. Make this plan specific and very detailed; and define each of the steps in between.

Exercise

Ask yourself, *what* jobs must I hold between now and then? *How* can I get these jobs, and *when*? *Who* will help? *What* will I have to learn? *How* am I going to learn these things?

In this planning, cite your job requirements, positions, training experience and education, and above all, the people who will necessarily be involved. To whom can you take this plan to get realistic feedback? Is your boss the person? Do you know anyone else who might help?

Now draw up a personal plan of action. On a sheet of paper fill in your particular goals at the top (do one goal at a time). Then, list these headings across the sheet:

Benefits	Problems and Obstacles	Potential Solutions	Target Date	Progress to Date

Under each heading, spell out in detail everything you can think of about your goal. List all the tangible and intangible benefits you'll enjoy when you reach your goal. Include not only things like increased income and status, but self-respect, greater freedom of expression, more confidence—anything that is meaningful to you.

Next, list all the problems and obstacles you'll probably encounter so you won't be surprised or frustrated when they occur. Then list all the possible solutions you can think of. Be creative here. If you're after a promotion, what do you need to learn? Who do you need to know? Who can help?

Finally, give yourself a realistic target date to help with your commitment for each step in your plan Then note your progress as you go along.

Just as a football player needs to know how many yards there are to go for a first down or a touchdown, you need to know what you have to do to get from where you are now to where you want to be, and when. Once you have this personal action plan, you'll have a clear picture of what behaviors you need to reach your goal.

At this stage, you have to begin to look for a coach, a mentor, an advocate, perhaps someone in a senior management position who can teach you, support you, advise you, criticize you. It is essential to present yourself as someone worth investing in, someone who can eventually make a return on the help you receive.

Now, re-evaluate your plan. Is it realistic in terms of total time commitment? Can you make it more realistic? Will it be rewarding enough to cover the personal costs you will have to pay?

This approach makes a tangible difference. Now you are *actively* working to further your career. You look motivated, promotable. You are beginning to control your career life.

Your Present Style of Behavior

Now let's look at your present style of behavior, as well as some ways to bring your style under your control.

When women are being interviewed for participation in human behavior skill seminars, they say things like this:

A government supervisor:

I've been here for ten years, and I'm good at my job. But they never offer me a promotion—only the men get the management jobs. One of these days, I'll report them to the EEO Officer.

A computer programmer:

I'm so confused, I don't know what I really want. I like my job—but I'd like to get married, too, and my future husband might not want a career wife. Women really get an unfair deal in this world.

An assistant insurance actuary:

I have a good job, and I like it. Besides, I don't know anything about promotion opportunities in this company. They never tell you anything. In this outfit, I'm lucky to be as far along as I am.

An executive secretary:

I'm really afraid to take another step. I don't know what's ahead, and I don't know how to find out. Suppose I took a bigger job, and had to deal with all the criticism and put-downs. I think I'd fall apart.

What are these women really doing? In a way, they are defending themselves and their self-concept. They have problems and they are using a defense called *projection*—they are blaming others for the condition of their own lives. Of course, sometimes women *are* victimized by others, by events, or by society—and they *do* have legitimate complaints. Often, however, blaming others can be a way of copping out on personal responsibility, and for the choices and decisions one has made in life.

Defensive Behavior and Coping Behavior

Now let's take a look at two ways of dealing with a situation—involving defensive behavior and coping behavior.[5] When you understand the difference between these two styles of behavior, you will begin to develop a knowledge of how you are dealing with others—effectively or ineffectively.

- To *cope* successfully is to deal positively with others, with reality, and to feel good about yourself.
- To *defend* is to pamper yourself in order to lessen the hurt caused by others and reality.
- Coping involves behaving: doing, saying, ACTING.
- Defending involves thinking, feeling, fantasy, planning, talking to yourself.
- When you cope successfully, you try to change the reality that is causing the bad feelings you have. Ask for a promotion. Find out what you need to do . . . take a chance!
- When you defend yourself, you try to change reality by pampering yourself—like taking a day off, or having another drink.

Examples

Let's look at a common situation, with both a defensive and a coping reaction. Then we'll discuss ways of coping and defending behavior in particular situations.

Martha is an accountant who sees herself as an expert. Naturally, she wants others to see her that way, too. Bill, a district sales manager, calls her and says, "Martha, the sales projections you did for my territory are all wrong. You'll have to do them over from scratch."

Of course, Martha doesn't think salespeople know *anything* about statistics. And she explodes in defensive anger. "What do you mean, wrong? You don't know *anything* about figures—I've forgotten more about sales forecasting than you'll ever know!"

Result: Martha doesn't get what she wants (to have others see her as an expert), and Bill doesn't get what he wants (an improved sales projection). He may also complain to Martha's boss.

Here is Martha's coping reaction to the same situation: "I'm sorry you feel that way. What specifically seems to be the problem?"

Result: Martha comes across as efficient and cool-headed, which is the image she wants to project—and the manager feels free to say, calmly, what's on his mind.

Defensive behavior has four characteristics. First, it boomerangs. Just as in Martha's first reaction, it gets you the exact opposite of what you want.

Second, it's exaggerated. Martha's anger is too intense for the situation, and once she cools down, she'll know it.

Third, defensive behavior is repetitive—it tends to become a habit, like being passive and letting others walk all over you. You know you are doing it, but somehow you're unable to stop.

Fourth, defensive behavior is aimed at feelings rather than reality. It doesn't confront the real problem—instead, others are blamed or attacked.

Suppose you have been passed over for a promotion twice. Instead of finding out what you need to do to get ahead, you keep silent and wait. Naturally, you expect to get your promotion next, and to have your boss appreciate you for being tolerant and patient. But the next promotion goes to someone else. You have been passed over again—AND YOU ARE FURIOUS! You charge into your boss's office and, near tears, you exclaim, "What do you mean by giving my promotion to someone else, after I've worked so hard and been so patient . . ."

That isn't likely to get you a promotion. In fact, your boss will probably think—or say—"Women are all the same—can't control their emotions!"

Your goals were (a) a promotion and (2) your boss's appreciation—but they boomeranged. You lost on both counts. Here's an alternative reaction—a coping reaction: You can say, "I realize you need to promote the person you feel is best qualified, but I am disappointed to be passed over, and I'd like to know what I have to do to qualify the next time."

With this response, you might not get the promotion, but at least you've let your boss know you want one, and you've done so in a calm, cool, and professional manner.

Coping means that you are actively changing something in reality—usually *your* behavior. Change the job. Speak up. Ask what promotions are open to you. Sometimes, of course, you may change *only* your feelings—but it's a constructive change to learn to *not* get emotional and upset about things you don't like.

Of course, with coping you run the risk of ending the relationship. You will almost certainly change the *quality* of the relationship. By using coping behavior, you indicated that you and the other person have a changed relationship—you no longer wish to be dependent, the "giver," the waiter."

Exercise

Do you cope or defend in certain situations? Let's see. Take the Coping vs. Defending Test (see Table 1.2).

TABLE 1.2
Coping vs. Defending Test

Your ability to draw others to you, or be "nourishing," is directly related to your level of defensive behavior. Generally, the more defensive you are—in both frequency and intensity—the less "nourishing" you are to others. Also, highly defensive behavior always produces the exact opposite response from that it seeks—in other words, it boomerangs. So, rather than drawing others to you, bringing you love, respect or whatever it is you seek, it invariably produces the opposite result.

In this test we ask you first to rate the *frequency* of your behavior in the following situations by making a checkmark under the appropriate column. Then, under the last column, rate the *intensity* of your reaction to each situation on a scale of 1 to 4 (1 means you are calm, 2 mildly concerned, 3 annoyed, and 4 very upset). And finally, take the *end result test* to learn the degree of boomerang your behavior may be producing.

	Frequency			
	Rarely	Occasionally	Usually	Intensity
1. People take advantage of me.	___	___	___	___
2. I worry about success or failure.	___	___	___	___
3. No matter how hard I try, men hurt me.	___	___	___	___
4. I fing it difficult to be my authentic, honest self.	___	___	___	___

TABLE 1.2 (Continued)

	Rarely	Occasionally	Usually	Intensity
5. I feel others don't recognize my potential.	——	——	——	——
6. I correct my family and friends.	——	——	——	——
7. I resent criticism from others.	——	——	——	——
8. Compliments embarrass me.	——	——	——	——
9. It's important to me that others approve of what I do.	——	——	——	——
10. I feel others should do what I expect of them.	——	——	——	——
11. Many people I deal with are unfair.	——	——	——	——
12. I tell little white lies or exaggerate the truth.	——	——	——	——
13. I make impulsive decisions.	——	——	——	——
14. When people do favors for me I suspect their motives.	——	——	——	——
15. I get upset if I don't get my own way.	——	——	——	——
16. I think I'm entitled to more than other people.	——	——	——	——
17. When something goes wrong, other people are to blame.	——	——	——	——
18. I feel bad when others forget my name or spell it wrong.	——	——	——	——
19. I criticize others, including strangers.	——	——	——	——
20. I'd rather be alone than meet strangers.	——	——	——	——
21. I avoid sticking my neck out in my relationships with others.	——	——	——	——
22. My interest in money comes first, regardless of other concerns.	——	——	——	——
23. I must justify my actions in pursuing my interests.	——	——	——	——
24. I don't feel skilled at sizing up other people.	——	——	——	——

TABLE 1.2 (Continued)

	Rarely	Occasionally	Usually	Intensity
25. I worry about feeling adequate to cope with life.	___	___	___	___
26. I feel that most people can't be trusted.	___	___	___	___
27. It's necessary for me to defend my past actions.	___	___	___	___
28. I feel it's important to impress others favorably.	___	___	___	___
29. I worry about the future.	___	___	___	___
30. It's important that others accept my point of view.	___	___	___	___
31. I express warm feelings only to close friends.	___	___	___	___
32. I feel appearance is of great importance.	___	___	___	___
33. I dislike having my weakness exposed.	___	___	___	___
34. I think most people are antagonistic.	___	___	___	___
35. I find it difficult to laugh at my troubles.	___	___	___	___
36. I regret and resent some things in the past.	___	___	___	___
37. I avoid embarrassment whenever I can.	___	___	___	___
38. I save good clothes for special occasions.	___	___	___	___
39. I don't express affection unless I'm sure it will be returned.	___	___	___	___
40. Other women annoy me.	___	___	___	___
41. I get angry and upset by small things.	___	___	___	___
42. If others disagree with me I get angry.	___	___	___	___
43. It saddens me the way others behave.	___	___	___	___
44. I believe that love can cure all things.	___	___	___	___

TABLE 1.2 (Continued)

	Rarely	Occasionally	Usually	Intensity
45. It makes me nervous to have others laugh when I don't know why.	——	——	——	——
46. If others stare at me I get embarrassed or nervous.	——	——	——	——
47. When I get angry it takes me a long time to get over it.	——	——	——	——
48. I get angry when someone keeps me waiting.	——	——	——	——
49. I feel left out and sad when I'm at a large gathering.	——	——	——	——
50. Meeting new people makes me feel uptight and withdrawn.	——	——	——	——

END RESULT TEST

All of us have the basic needs to love and be loved and to feel self-worth. This is the reality of being human. Therefore, study those situations which you've rated **usually**. Then study those situations which you've rated 4 in **intensity**. Then check out the boomerang effect by asking yourself the following questions:

  A. In those situations which I have checked *usually* and/or 4 in *intensity*, do I end up being loved or unloved because of my behavior?
  B. Does my behavior in these situations produce the result(s) I really want? (That is, does it draw others to you?)
  C. Do I like and value myself for my behavior in these situations? Or would I really like to behave differently?

Generally, if your answer to A is "unloved"; if your answer to B is that your behavior doesn't produce the results you really want; and if your answer to C is that you'd really like to behave differently but you continue without changing, then in fact you may be devaluing yourself and producing much of your own unhappiness.

Ultimate Responsibility

Now let's look at the concept of *ultimate responsibility*. Ultimate responsibility means that as an adult you, and you alone, are responsible for your choices, your feelings, and your behavior. That's right—unless you are physically overpowered, you are responsible for everything that happens to you. And, although you may find this idea frightening, remember: you live with the results of your choices and behavior. Yes, your power to choose is the most awesome power you have—because by accepting responsibility for your choices, you put yourself in control of your life.

Examples

Here are some of the ways people deny responsibility for themselves:
A secretary:

I work for the world's meanest boss. He always criticizes me and I can't help it if I break down and cry.

She chooses to cry. There are many other things she could do. And she is denying her responsibility. Chances are her boss's criticism is not without some reason. And even if she is *not* at fault, she doesn't have to respond with crying, at least in front of him.
A saleswoman:

I hate this rat race and I hate this company. But I have to have a job and this is all I know how to do.

She could choose to get a new job, of course. But she could also choose to stay where she is and stop feeling that way. She doesn't *have* to hate it; she chooses to do so. She could also choose to learn what she needs to do to move into another, better job.
A supervisor:

My subordinates can't do anything right or on time. I have to stay late and do it for them. They are driving me crazy.

She could choose to insist on competent work, of course. And she could *also* choose to stop going crazy.

As I have said, once we become adults, everything we do—unless we are physically overpowered—is our *own* choice. We choose to live where we do; we choose to stay in the work we do; we choose a mate and then choose to maintain or destroy the relationship; we choose to be fat or thin, sober or drunk; we choose all our relationships with others. And we choose our emotional responses and feelings—like anger, depression, shyness, withdrawal, and the like. Once in discussing this in a seminar, a participant took sharp issue with me:

> Wait a minute! Are you trying to tell me that when I ask for a promotion and my boss says, "That's a man's job. Be a good girl and stick to your own job," he doesn't make *me* feel bad? That's for the birds!

Then another woman spoke up:

> Yes, and *you* ought to spend an hour giving performance reviews to my staff. If I don't give them top marks, they hate me. I feel terrible!

Are these valid objections? Let's take a closer look. I say feelings are not just emotions that happen to you. Feelings are reactions you choose to have. Let's see how this works.

First, you and you alone control your thoughts. They are your own, uniquely yours. No one else can get inside your head—it is your brain, and no one else can control what you think.

Second, your feelings come from your thoughts. You cannot have a feeling without first experiencing a thought. Without your brains you can't feel anything. Someone's death doesn't make you unhappy—you can't be unhappy until you learn about the death. And bosses and subordinates don't make you feel bad—it's your *thoughts* about rejection and disapproval which do it.

Third, if you control your thoughts, and your feelings come from thoughts, then you are able to control your feelings by working on your thoughts. Simply put, you may believe that people or events make you feel bad, but this is not so. Your *thoughts* about them make you unhappy. Once you change your thoughts, new feelings emerge, and you will have taken another step on the road to personal freedom.

Yes, the question is not whether you *can* control your feelings, but if you *will*. And if you decide not to, remember it means that you hand over to others the right to control how you feel—in effect, pull your strings.

When you do take responsibility for your choices and for your feelings, how will it help you in managing?

For one thing, you won't waste time being afraid of rejection, disapproval, or failure. And this freedom will give you time to concentrate on things you need to learn to do your job well—which means making new decisions for your life.

The first and most important decision is, Are you for or against yourself?

Do you want to make a new decision to change, to grow, and to throw out all of the negative attitudes that hold you back and make you look bad?

If you decide you want to help yourself, you can choose to do the things that make you look good, instead of the things that make you look bad.

Exercise

Go back and study your Coping vs. Defending Test. Circle the things you do that you believe may cause you problems in your work and in your relationships with others. Then, for each problem area, do the End Result Test.

Now, what do you do with this information? *First*, accept it. Remember, there is always a good reason for whatever you do, particularly if you are trying to meet your basic needs of love and self-worth. Once you accept your behavior, you'll be able to see why you have been using it. Then, with your own acceptance and understanding, you can decide whether or not you want to change. And if you don't want to change, that's fine. In which case, look at your behavior and say: ''That's my behavior. That's the way I do it, and I love myself for it.''

However, if you decide you want to stop the behavior, then make the change and make it *in reality*. For example, suppose you have a habit of making critical and sarcastic remarks that devalue peers and subordinates and make them resent you. Stop all such remarks for a significant period of time—a day at first . . . then a week . . . then a month . . . then longer, until you have eliminated the behavior.

Next, check out your feelings about your new behavior. Are your feelings changed? What is your feedback to yourself? Do you like yourself better now?

Finally, check out your feedback from others. Have they changed? Do they smile more, seem to trust and like you more? Do they value you? If not, something is still wrong.

If that's the case, go back to Step 1 and repeat the process.

SUM-UP

Yes, it can be a long process. Facing reality and growing as a human being is painful. Few of us like to admit we are wrong. But there is a great deal we can change and can do if we use coping behavior rather than defending behavior, and if we take the responsibility for our behavior. We can forget about pinning the blame somewhere else . . . forget about trying to get even . . . and get on with making positive, creative new choices for our lives that will bring us more of what we need.

And that is reality: You *can* thrown out all the negative garbage. You *can* make new choices. You *are* responsible. And you *can* do it.

2

Women and Men Are Different . . . But the *Job* Is the Same

In the Introduction, I mentioned briefly that as a woman you have developed some special skills which men aren't usually encouraged to develop. These special skills can give you a powerful advantage in managing others. But you also have some learned behaviors, fears, habits, and conditioning which can hurt you. In this chapter we'll examine these positives and negatives—first, to make you consciously aware of them; second, so you can learn to strengthen the positives and overcome the negatives.

We'll also look at the difference in typical male and female organizational behavior. This will help you understand how you may be seen by senior managers. We'll also discuss the *functions* of managers—whether they are women or men—so you can get an understanding of what skills you need in a managerial position. Then, as you progress through the book, you'll be learning how to combine your assets as a woman and your knowledge about managerial responsibilities to become a superior manager.

THE POSITIVES AND
THE NEGATIVES OF BEING
"TRAINED" AS A FEMALE

The same early conditioning that made so many women passive, noncompetitive, tongue-tied, thin-skinned, emotional, and afraid of taking risks also gave women some valuable skills. Most women have learned how to be empathetic, warm, sensitive to others, caring, and generous. We understand and express feelings. And probably most important, we listen well. Too often, we use these skills until we get to be managers. Then, something strange happens. We forget our skills. We may freeze, and become unresponsive. We may find ourselves unable to exercise authority. We may compensate for our fears by becoming pushy, loud, disagreeably aggressive. We may turn into prying busybodies in the mistaken idea that we are showing interest in our subordinates. Many of us become over-generous, and feel we must do anything to please. We won't speak up, and thus we wind up being victimized by others. And finally, there are those of us who come apart emotionally.

At one time or another I've played most of these roles and so have most of the successful women I know. Lenore Hershey, editor of *Ladies Home Journal*, and one of the most influential women in America, once told me:

> I came to power rather late in my career—I was a grandmother, in fact. The first year I felt like I was dressed in my mother's clothes, sitting behind Daddy's desk. The second year, I became so obnoxious I made enemies I still have. Only after three years did I feel comfortable enough with power to say to someone who opposed an idea of mine, "Do it anyway because I'm the editor and that's the way I want it!"

Our negative behaviors stem mostly from our early conditioning: our "little ladies don't . . ." and "people won't like you if . . ." training. When you get into a position in which you need to exercise power and get things done through other people, this conditioning gets in your way. You're uncomfortable about your new role, and you may react by playing either mouse or bully. Either way, you're using defensive behavior. And one thing you can count on is that defensive behavior doesn't work—it produces the exact opposite of what you seek. What, then, is the solution? It's one thing to say, "I won't be defensive" . . . it's quite another to *act* on this resolve.

Valuing Yourself

How do you avoid defensive behavior? The answer is that you learn the skills for *valuing yourself*. These skills add up to learning to take responsibility for yourself, your feelings, your behavior, and being good to yourself.

You make all your choices. The first thing to remember is that no one can make you feel anything or do anything if you don't allow it to happen. As we've seen, you as an adult are free to make all of your choices and decisions—unless someone has a gun at your head.

Your behavior and feelings are learned. The second thing to remember is that all of your behavior and feelings were learned, and this includes negative things like feeling shy, nervous, inadequate, and unhappy. That's important because it means that negative behaviors can be *un*learned and that you can learn new ways to feel and respond.

Self-respect leads to respect for others. Finally, when you do take good care of your *self*—when you learn self-respect, dignity, assurance—you can build positive relationships with others based on trust, warmth, compassion, openness, and respect—instead of on manipulation.

Rules for Valuing Yourself

What are the rules for learning to value yourself?

Rule 1: Don't demand perfection from yourself. Set realistic goals that you *can* and *want* to achieve.

Rule 2: Reward, comfort, and love yourself. You're OK!

Rule 3: Realize that you have the right to decide who and what you want to be without making excuses, justifying, or apologizing. You don't need everyone else's approval . . . and you certainly won't get it. It's your life and what happens in it is up to you.

Rule 4: Refuse to be manipulated by other people's greed, helplessness, or anger. Set limits. Say "no" when you mean no. And confront those who try to manipulate you by saying "you should."

Rule 5: Check out your "should's." Sure, there are things you *have* to do, like paying your bills. That's reality. But these are not "should's." How about the idea that you should always be friendly to your subordinates? What's the basis of this "should"? Check it out. You may find that believing such a notion and trying to act on it *don't* make you a good manager.

Rule 6: Recognize feelings of inadequacy, fear, and guilt for what they are—legacies from your parents and other adults. You can decide *not* to have those feelings.

Rule 7: Be constructively selfish. In the long run, doing what is best for you is usually best for everyone concerned. Remember that no matter what you do, someone is not going to like it—so you have to risk being disliked, or even ending relationships, if you are going to function in your best interests.

Rule 8: Recognize that there are limits to your power. You control no more than 50% of any relationship—your half. You can't get inside anyone else's head—nor they yours. So it is best to express your feelings and your doubts. If somebody says "Do this" and you don't understand, say so. Too often we pretend that we understand so we won't look bad.

Rule 9: Don't answer questions you don't want to answer. Questions are often threatening, demanding, manipulative—especially the WHY or WHY NOT questions. There is no rule that you must answer questions.

Rule 10: Stay in the here and now and cope with reality. If you blame others or the world for your problems . . . if you live in the past or in the future . . . or if your behavior is aimed at making you *feel better* instead of *solving your problems* . . . you are defending instead of coping. Every healthy person has problems—and you do have the ability to cope with them.

OK I know these kinds of rules may seem a bit outrageous. But they involve *real* choices you have to make for your life. You can accept them or reject them. That's up to you. But whatever you do, keep in mind that it's your choice—because you *live with the results* . . . and you don't have to justify or explain your choices to anyone.

I think that learning to value myself was the most important lesson I ever learned. And I know that once you start to understand how to value yourself, you will see positive changes in both your professional and personal life.

Valuing Yourself Helps You as a Manager

How can learning to value yourself help you to be a skilled manager? First, you will automatically stop most of the defensive behaviors that prevent you from dealing with others effectively . . . you can't be a mouse or a bully and value yourself at the same time. Therefore, you'll be able to stop the negative behaviors that hurt you and get on with the job.

Second, you will learn to really value *others*. And in today's organizational world, this is vital. You cannot manage others without valuing and respecting them.

Impact of Your Behavior on Others

To understand this concept of learning to value oneself, let's take a look at the tremendous impact your behavior can have on your subordinates, peers, and superiors.

An interview with Carol:

> I'm an associate editor for a publisher. I'm unmarried, 31 years old, and not too certain what I want to do for the rest of my life. I do my job well, but I don't kill myself. Six months ago, I was offered a job as editor of a small magazine, but I turned it down because I thought I wasn't ready for it. Now I'm sorry, but I'm afraid that if I talk to my boss about it he'll be furious—or else think I'm a little crazy.

An interview with Carol's boss:

> Carol—yes she's a good editor, but not too—uh—motivated, you know. I honestly can't figure her out. She doesn't get along with the men. Frankly, she's kind of bitchy. Last fall I offered her a promotion—and would you believe it, she turned it down. Said she wasn't ready . . . but I think it was a copout. She's either lazy—or scared. Maybe both.

Can you see what Carol is doing to herself? Because her goals are fuzzy, she's not too easy to get along with, won't take risks, and is passive. She's digging herself into a dead-end job. Now, here's an exchange between Helen and her boss:

BOSS: Helen, this piece of copy won't fly. There's no powerful selling theme to it. Let's talk it over.

HELEN: I don't agree with you at all.

BOSS: Now Helen, don't get upset. I'm trying to help you.

HELEN: (upset) I'm not upset. It just seems to me that you're too critical of my work.

BOSS: (tough) I have to be critical—it's my job. I know you're trying, but this is way off the mark. Go re-think it and . . .

HELEN: (in tears) Oh, Mr. Davis, I just can't think about it now. I worked so hard on that copy, I can't believe you're saying what you're saying . . .

Poor Helen. She's upset from the criticism and reduced to tears. Of course, because of her conditioning, she's learned it's OK to express her feelings—and, of course, it is. But not in front of her boss or peers. How much better for her future if she had "remembered" an important call, and then done her crying in private . . . or better, if she had expressed her disappointment and emotion in a better way.

OVERCOMING THE NEGATIVES OF BEING TRAINED AS A WOMAN

The basic requirements for success in any organization are clear—realistic goals; a drive to achieve; the ability to get along well with others, to compete, to be flexible, and to take calculated risks. That's the way it is—in every successful organization. These are the skills most men learn before they are 10 years old—and which most women *don't* learn. You have to learn them, because there is no sense in centering your hopes on the way things *should* be; you need to deal with the way things *are*. And it is never too late to learn. In the first chapter we discussed the key issue of setting clear, realistic goals. Here are some other things you need to learn in order to be a good manager within a male-dominated organization. Men who are moving up in organizations do these things automatically and this is what senior managers look for when they are seeking out the "promotables" in the organization.

1. You need to stop waiting to be chosen, invited, persuaded, asked to accept a promotion. Start acting. Let people know what you want and what you're prepared to do to get it. To gain visibility, you need to let others see you going after a promotion and working for it. Remember, *no one can see your feelings*. You have to behave as if you *want* to achieve success.

2. You need to stop waiting to be told what to do. Take the initiative. Ask to learn new skills. Ask to be given new assignments. Ask to take on new projects. This behavior helps you in three important ways: it shows you are motivated, it shows you like to compete for new opportunities, and it shows you are willing to take some risks by learning new things.

3. You need to stop being afraid to take risks. If you're afraid of risks, ask yourself why. Do you see risks only as losing propositions or as uncontrollable gambles rather than as manageable acts? Have you ever thought of risk-taking as something you can *control?*

Exercise

Think about a career-related risk you might take. Then make two lists. First, list the positives that might result from taking a risk. Then, in the second list, write down the things that could go wrong. Do your lists tend to balance one another? Does one list or the other seem stronger? Put some odds on your entries. How possible, probable, likely, certain do they seem? Why? What might you do to increase the degree of certainty or decrease it where you don't want it? In other words, how can you begin to deal realistically with your own assumptions about risk?

4. Finally, you need to manage your emotions and become less vulnerable to criticism. Many people believe that when women are under pressure, criticized, or attacked, they will fall apart and cry. And there is a lot of truth in this. Women do express feelings more freely. Yet men see crying—in front of other people—as the mark of someone who is uncontrolled . . ., i.e., someone you can't trust. So, if you do want a career, you'll have to learn to manage your emotions.

Henning and Jardim, in *The Managerial Woman*, offer this approach:

First, sit down and think back over the last few years. What kinds of situations caused you to feel or become emotionally upset? Write them down. Describe what happened; where you were, what the setting was, who was involved, what was said, and what—as precisely as you can describe it—made you feel so angry or so vulnerable that you broke down in tears. After you've written this down look for patterns in what you've written. Is there a pattern in terms of time? Or is there a pattern in terms of the people involved? Did it tend to happen when you were criticized? When you were challenged? When you felt left out? The more you can understand about why it happened in the past, the more you can anticipate when it may happen in the future—and this is the first step toward managing it.

If you can begin to predict for example when, in what kinds of situations, under what kinds of pressures you are likely to cry, you can begin to deal with it by recognizing the signals and acting before it happens. You can remember that you have an important phone call coming in to your office and your secretary isn't there. You can simply excuse yourself for a moment and, in privacy, you can either pull yourself together, drink a glass of cold water (which helps) or go ahead and be upset.[1]

[1]Margaret Henning and Anne Jardim, *The Managerial Woman* (Garden City, New York: Anchor Press/Doubleday, 1977) pp. 177–78.

Dealing with Criticism

Now let's talk about criticism. Taking criticism personally is related to the need for other people's approval. Of course, you do need approval for what you *do*—performance is the name of the game. But this is not the same as needing approval for who you *are*. When you interpret criticism as a personal failure instead of as a comment on a piece of work, you become terribly vulnerable. Then, too often you'll be unable to take appropriate action to correct the problem and get on with the job. There are several good ways to handle criticism and judgment in a less personal way. Let's examine them.

You define yourself. One way is to stop depending on other people's approval for defining who you are. Your self-worth is not related to what you do, or whether you succeed or fail, or to other people's opinions of you. Your self-worth is the value you ascribe to *you*.

Of course, everyone enjoys compliments, appreciation, and praise. We all like applause. The problem comes when we *need* it to operate . . . or if we fall apart when we are criticized. So you need to separate criticism of what you do from who you are.

Dr. Wayne Dyer, in his book *Your Erroneous Zones*, offers the following advice:

> Take a look at the way the world works. To put it succinctly, you can never please everyone In fact, if you please fifty percent of the people you are doing quite well. This is no secret. You know that at least half of the people in your world are going to disagree with at least half the things you say. If this is accurate (and you need only look at landslide elections to see that forty-four percent of the population still voted against the winner), then you will always have about a 50–50 chance of getting some disapproval whenever you express an opinion.
>
> Armed with this knowledge, you can begin to look at disapproval in a new light. When someone disapproves of something you say, instead of being hurt, or instantly shifting your opinion to gain praise, you can remind yourself that you've just run into one of those folks in the fifty percent who don't agree with you.[2]

Yes, once you expect disapproval, you won't be surprised or hurt by

[2]Dr. Wayne W. Dyer, *Your Erroneous Zones* (New York: Funk & Wagnall's Inc., 1976), p. 63.

it—and you'll stop making other people's views of you more important than *your* opinion of you.

You can give yourself credit.   Another way to become less vulnerable to criticism is to start feeling good about accomplishments, and praise yourself for them. This gives you a balance against negative judgments and put-downs. Of course, it isn't always easy, because women have been trained not to feel too proud. But once you realize that nothing bad will happen when you praise yourself, you'll start to feel better about your behavior.

Here's how to start giving yourself credit: examine the most routine things you do, to see if you do them well. There are probably very few people who can do your job as well as you can, whether it's writing a report, selling real estate, or balancing accounts. How about your hobbies? Chances are you're better than other people at some hobby—tennis, gardening, photography, or painting. Think of all the people who can't write a decent sentence, carry a tune, or draw a straight line. All of these can be sources of feeling good about yourself. So relish your successful experiences. Give yourself a mental pat on the back—or even a small reward—for them.

Don't put yourself down.   And avoid judging yourself negatively and putting yourself down. It does little good to compare yourself with other people. They may be better than you in some areas, but they have their weaknesses, too—often weaknesses you can't see. Many people are brash on the outside, but insecure inside; all you are able to see is the surface brashness. Some are smooth on the job, but all thumbs on the tennis court. All you can see is the strengths, not the weaknesses. If someone is better than you in one area, what difference does it make? You're probably better in another. Don't worry about it. Remember, no one is perfect.

Fogging: A Tool

If you are especially vulnerable to criticism, here is a good tool to help you overcome this negative trait. It is called *Fogging* and to my knowledge was first described by Dr. Manuel J. Smith in *When I Say No, I Feel Guilty.*[3]

[3]Dr. Manuel J. Smith, *When I Say No, I Feel Guilty* (New York: The Dial Press, 1975), pp. 97–98.

Imagine a fog bank. It is thick and pervasive. You cannot clearly see through it. But it offers no resistance. If you throw a rock at it, the rock won't ricochet back, allowing you to pick it up and throw it at the fog once more. Any rock you throw goes right through it, and the fog is unaffected. Inevitably, you'll give up trying to change or attack the fog and leave it alone. You can't manipulate it.

When you are criticized, you can cope assertively by *fogging*— offering no resistance or hard psychological striking surfaces for any critical statements thrown at you.

Fogging is a very useful skill to have—for two reasons. First, it makes you feel better because it reduces your defensive responses to criticism and personal attack. When you practice this skill, you no longer feel guilty, anxious, inadequate, or frightened.

Second, fogging cuts the emotional puppet strings which make us automatically react—at times with panic—to personal attack from others. Overreacting to personal attack causes us to be manipulated into *defending* what we want to do instead of *doing* it.

Uses of fogging.   Here are the three ways to use fogging. First, you can agree with any truth in the critical statements of others. For example, your boss says, "If you didn't spend so much time talking on the phone, you could do more around here." You can "fog" by agreeing with any truth in the criticism: "You're right. I *could* do more around here."

The next way to use fogging is to agree with any *possible* truth. Suppose your boss keeps after you: "Furthermore, if you'd put forth a little more effort, *I* wouldn't have to work so hard." You can "fog" with a possible or probable truth: "You could be right. I might be able to take more of the load off your shoulders."

Finally, you can use fogging by agreeing with the general truth when others try to manipulate you with logical statements. If the boss says, "You know how important it is to the company's profits for every employee to be 100 percent motivated and productive. If all the employees worked as little as you do, we'd be out of business!" You can "fog" by agreeing with the logic of the statement: "That certainly makes good sense. Motivation and more productivity are essential to greater profits."

Exercise

Now we'd like you to practice this skill. Table 2.1 contains critical statements for you to respond to with fogging responses. To each of these statements, respond by either agreeing with any truth, agreeing with the possibilities, or agreeing with the general truth.

Exercise

Another way to practice this skill is to *role-play*. Get a friend to make critical remarks to you for 2 minutes and practice fogging. Then change roles and you criticize your friend. This will help you become skilled at fogging; it will also help you experience how difficult it is to keep criticizing someone who is not defending his or her position.

USING THE POSITIVES
OF BEING TRAINED AS A WOMAN

Now let's look at the positive side—the strengths, behaviors, and qualities you bring to the manager's job *because* you have been "trained" as a woman.

Listening

First, and probably most important, most women listen well. Many men don't listen well—in fact, they try to overcontrol others by talking too much. This is one of their most serious liabilities. So even though you may think of your listening skill as negative or nonassertive, used right, it can give you a powerful advantage in a manager's job.

TABLE 2.1
Fogging
===

Fog the following critical statements. Agree with any truth, any possible truth, or any logic. Don't defend yourself, just tell the other person that you agree, while continuing to value yourself. For example, if a man says, "You're a typical woman," respond, "You may be right. I am pretty typical,"

TABLE 2.1 (Continued)

or "I can see how you think I'm typical," *not* "I don't see what's wrong with being typical.' "

1. You don't care if I have to work late to help you out. You could at least feel guilty.

___

2. You shouldn't wear pants. You don't want people to think you're unfeminine, do you?

___

3. You seem scared to death whenever you have to make a presentation.

___

4. You have too much makeup on, as usual.

___

5. You're too careless.

___

6. That hat looks like a raven after it flew into a fan. Where did you get that awful thing?

___

7. If you paid attention when I gave you instructions, you wouldn't have to bother me with questions.

___

8. You're just like every other dumb broad.

___

9. All you do is talk, talk, talk.

___

10. That's a stupid idea.

___

11. You women are all the same—too emotional.

___

TABLE 2.1 (Continued)

12. You were late with the proposal and we lost the account.

Sample Fogging Response

1. You're right. I guess I could feel guiltier.
2. You're probably right. There are people who think wearing pants is unfeminine.
3. It's true. I am nervous when I make a presentation.
4. That's right. I do have my usual amount of makeup on.
5. You're probably right. I could be more careful.
6. You could be right. It does look something like a mutilated raven.
7. That may be true, I could pay closer attention.
8. That's true. I am a woman—so I am like them.
9. You're right, I do talk a lot.
10. You may be right. Perhaps it does need work.
11. That's true, women are more emotional than men.
12. You're probably right, we lost the account because I was late.

Reprinted by courtesy of Learning Dynamics, Inc.

The amount of misunderstandings, mistakes, opportunities lost, and time wasted because people don't really listen is mind-boggling. Listening is the cornerstone of good communication—one of the all-important "people skills" we'll discuss shortly. And it is also one of the most valuing, rewarding, important gifts one human being can give to another. Later on, we'll see why valuing others is the surest way to succeed in managing people. But isn't it exciting to know you are already good at this important skill? And when you finish the book you'll be an expert!

Empathy

You have other strengths and assets that can help you as a manager. Like most women, you have a lot of natural empathy and warmth. You give people your full attention, try to understand them, and see things from their point of view. And you understand and value *feelings*. Because of this, people usually trust you. And trust is what attitude, effort, performance, and productivity are all about.

Building trust is a *skill*, and you probably already have this skill, as well as other important skills that are essential for managing people. Once you learn to sharpen these skills, overcome your negative conditioning, and learn how to handle the specific tasks of managing, you'll possess all you need to be a superior manager.

FUNCTIONS OF MANAGERS

Now let's take a look at what managers do. First, there is the classic view that has influenced management principles since French industrialist Henri Fayol first introduced it in 1916.

Fayol: Management Functions

Fayol believed that the good manager has four basic functions:[4]

1. Planning
2. Organizing
3. Measuring
4. Controlling

If you *ask* a manager what he or she does, these are the steps that will probably be cited. But if you watch what that person does, you may have a difficult time relating what you see to these four functions. They really indicate *objectives* most managers have for themselves when they work.

Mintzberg: Roles of the Manager

There is a newer way of defining a manager's job, developed by Henry Mintzberg at McGill University in Canada.

[4]Henri Fayol, *General and Industrial Management* (London, England: Sir Isaac Pitman & Sons, 1949).

The manager is that person in charge of an organization or one of its sub-units. Besides chief executive officers, this definition would include vice presidents, bishops, head nurses, division heads, and prime ministers. Can all of these people have anything in common? Indeed they can. For an important starting point, all are vested with formal authority over an organizational unit. From formal authority comes status, which leads to various interpersonal relations, and from these comes access to information. Information, in turn, enables the manager to make decisions and strategies for his [or her] unit.[5]

Mintzberg describes the manager's job in terms of ten "roles," or organized sets of behaviors identified with a position.[6] He defines these ten roles as a Gestalt—an integrated whole whose parts are interwoven and fairly inseparable. Three of the ten roles arise directly from the manager's formal authority and involve basic interpersonal relationships:

1. *Figurehead*. By virtue of his or her position as head of an organizational unit, the manager must perform some duties of a ceremonial nature. The president greets the touring dignitaries, the supervisor attends the wedding of a lathe operator, and the sales manager takes an important customer to lunch.

2. *Leader*. Some of the activities connected with this role involve direct leadership. For example, in most organizations the manager is normally responsible for hiring and training the staff. In addition, every manager must motivate and encourage employees, somehow reconciling their individual needs with the goals of the organization.

3. *Liaison*. In this role the manager makes contacts outside the vertical chain of command. Managers spend as much time with peers and with people outside their units as they do with their own subordinates—and, surprisingly, very little time with their own superiors. Managers cultivate such contacts largely to find information.

The processing of information is a key part of the manager's job. There are three informational roles in managerial work:

4. *Monitor*. As *monitor*, the manager perpetually scans his/her environment for information, interrogates liaison contacts and subordinates, and receives unsolicited information, much of it as a result of the network of personal contacts. A good part of the information managers collect in the

---

[5]Henry Mintzberg, "The Manager's Job: Folklore and Fact," *Harvard Business Review*, July/August, 1975, pp. 54–59. Copyright © 1975 by the President and Fellows of Harvard College; all rights reserved.

[6]Ibid.

monitor role arrives in verbal form, often as gossip, hearsay, and speculation. By virtue of their contacts, managers have a natural advantage in collecting this soft information for the organization.

5. *Disseminator*. The manager shares and distributes information. She/he passes some of this privileged information directly to subordinates, who would otherwise have no access to it. When subordinates lack easy contact with one another, the manager will sometimes pass information from one to another.

6. *Spokesperson*. In this role the manager sends some information to people outside his/her unit—a president makes a speech to lobby for an organization cause, or a supervisor suggests a product modification to a supplier. In addition, as spokesperson, every manager informs and satisfies the influential people who control the organizational unit. For the supervisor, this may simply involve keeping the plant manager informed about the flow of work through the shop.

Decision-making Role.   Information is not, of course, an end in itself; it is the basic input to decision-making. The manager's major role is decision-making. Four roles describe the manager as decision-maker:

7. *Entrepreneur*. As entrepreneur, the manager seeks to improve the unit, to help it adapt to changing conditions in the environment.

8. *Disturbance-Handler*. In this role the manager responds to pressures. Here, change is beyond the manager's control. He or she must act because the pressures of the situation are too severe to be ignored: a strike looms, a major customer has gone bankrupt, or a supplier reneges on a contract.

9. *Resource-Allocator*. The manager decides who will get what in the organizational unit. The manager also designs the unit's structure, that pattern of relationships which determines how work is to be divided and coordinated. Also, in the role as resource-allocator, the manager authorizes the important decisions of his/her unit before they are implemented.

10. *Negotiator*. Negotiations are often routine, but they can't be avoided—they are an integral part of the job. Only the manager has the authority to commit organizational resources in "real time," and only the manager has the nerve-center information that important negotiations require.

As you can see, all of these roles involve *other people*—often those you may not like—as well as teamwork, tradeoffs, risk-taking, problem-solving, and communicating. (See summary in Figure 2.1.)

In later chapters, we'll cover some specific skills for setting goals for subordinates, organizing work, communicating, handling conflicts, and scientific problem-solving and decision-making. And we'll put heavy emphasis on teaching you the all-important *people* skills. But let's stay with you for now.

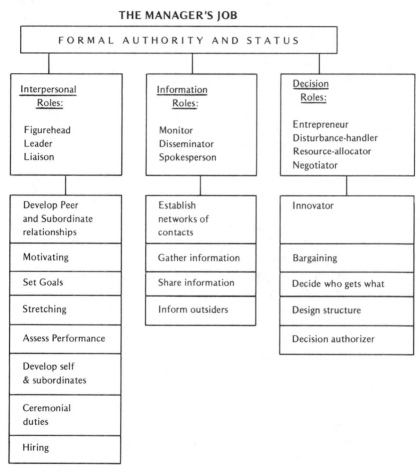

Figure 2.1   The Manager's Job

Reprinted by courtesy of Learning Dynamics, Inc. Based on material from "The Manager's Job" by Henry Mintzberg in *Harvard Business Review*, July-August, 1975.

SUM-UP

As you can see, the job of managing is the same for both men and women. The manager works with a special resource: people. And human beings are a unique resource, requiring special management skills.

And therein lies the problem for women who want to be successful managers: the job is the same, but in many ways women are different from men. You can easily learn how to conduct an interview, how to provide feedback, how to delegate, stretch (see pp. 63–64), and reward subordinates. But when all is said and done, relating with others and developing people—yourself included—is not just a matter of learning how to do specific tasks. It demands understanding and the ability to meet basic human needs—and it demands the ability to manage your environment and yourself.

You've already learned some ways to do this, and you'll learn a great deal more throughout this book. These skills will help you get over your negative habits and learn to capitalize on your natural strengths. Then you can be yourself. Don't try to be anyone but you. You aren't a man, so don't make the mistake of trying to act like one—or to act any phony role that does not reflect the authentic person you are. You are different. You are unique. Be *yourself*.

3
The
High Achiever
Leadership Style

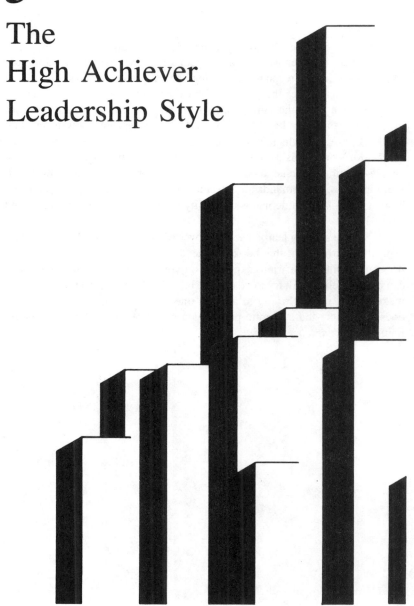

YOUR LEADERSHIP STYLE

Human behavior science has been with us for a very short time. But the findings from this field, which researches why human beings think, feel, and behave the way they do, have greatly improved our understanding of human motivation and achievement.

In this chapter, we will discuss the findings of a number of human behavior scientists (McGregor, McClelland, Likert, Atkinson, Argyris, Horowitz, to name a few) that apply to managing others successfully. It is a set of skills and techniques that we call the *high achiever leadership style*.

The high achiever leadership style is one that utilizes certain behavior in managing others . . . behavior that values people and meets basic human needs. This behavior communicates with, challenges, and rewards subordinates. It gives people room to move, allows them to take responsibility for doing their jobs, and gives them freedom to take intelligent risks and make mistakes without fear of being punished.

Because the high achiever leadership style meets human needs, it creates an organizational climate that triggers motivation striving.[1] On the other hand, the traditional leadership styles, formal (highly structured and power-oriented) and informal (loosely structured and affiliation-oriented), deny human needs and create a climate which kills motivation striving.

Therefore, in my view, the interdependent goals of high employee motivation and organizational success rest on the climate of the organization. And this climate is created by the leadership style of managers.

[1]Reprinted by courtesy of Learning Dynamics, Inc., from the "4 Dimension Leadership" program, Session I, 1975.

Today, most managers operate on a combination of the formal/ informal style. For this reason, learning to operate as a high achiever may demand some major, and perhaps difficult, changes in attitude and behavior. But learning this style of leadership will enable you to both grow as a manager and earn the respect and cooperation of those you manage.

But before we begin, let's find out what your personal style of leadership is.

Exercise

Complete the test of leadership style (Table 3.1).

TABLE 3.1
Leadership Style Test

Circle those items that apply to you as a leader. If a statement does not apply to you, do not circle it.

1. I believe in maintaining clear lines of authority.
2. I set high standards and hold workers accountable.
3. I encourage innovation on all levels.
4. I make my employees stick closely to the rules.
5. I never criticize a worker for a mistake.
6. I reward exceptional performance.
7. I try to establish a relaxed, easygoing atmosphere.
8. I want all my workers to be friendly, without any conflicts.
9. I remain aloof from my workers.
10. I encourage moderate risk-taking.
11. I think consistency is more important than creativity.
12. I want decisions to be made democratically in my organization.
13. I try to help my workers with their personal problems.
14. I give my workers maximum responsibility.
15. I want a sober atmosphere in my organization.

Scoring

Formal Style: Score one point for each of statements 1, 4, 9, 11, and 15 you circled.
Informal Style: Score one point for each of statements 5, 7, 8, 12, and 13 you circled.
Achievement Style: Score one point for each of statements 2, 3, 6, 10, and 14 you circled.
For any of the three leadership styles your total score means:
4 to 5 points: You are high in this style.

TABLE 3.1 (Continued)

2 to 3 points: You are moderate in this style.
0 to 1 point: You are very low in this style.

Part 2: Your Behavior Pattern in One-on-One Relationships

For each of the following situations, circle the letter that is closest to the way you would respond.

1. An employee who has been doing a fair job asks you how he or she has been doing.
   a. You're concerned about your performance.
   b. Do you think you can do better?
   c. You haven't been doing well.
   d. You have a tough job.
   e. I'm fed up with your mediocre performance.

2. A subordinate praises an idea of yours that you don't think is that good.
   a. What do you think is so good about it?
   b. I didn't think it was that good.
   c. I understand why you think you have to say it's good.
   d. You don't really think it's that good, do you?
   e. You liked my idea.

3. A subordinate complains that other employees have been making fun of her/him
   a. You must be doing something to deserve that.
   b. That's terrible!
   c. That's your problem, not mine.
   d. You seem upset because they make fun of you.
   e. How about ignoring it?

4. An employee, aged 62, wants to take early retirement.
   a. It must be tough to be old.
   b. You might as well retire, the way you're slowing up.
   c. You feel this would be a good time for you to retire.
   d. Why do you want to retire?
   e. Retire? I thought you were in your 20's.

TABLE 3.1 (Continued)

5. A subordinate tells you he/she finds his/her job dull.
   a. I don't care how you feel about it; just do it.
   b. You're bored by your job.
   c. How can we change your job to make it less dull?
   d. You shouldn't complain when the company is so good to you.
   e. I'm sorry the job is so dull.

6. A secretary tells you she has trouble handling her workload because she can't say "no" to any request.
   a. You feel overwhelmed because you can't refuse anyone.
   b. You can say "no" if you try.
   c. You shouldn't be so passive.
   d. They shouldn't make so many requests of you.
   e. You'll just have to work faster.

7. An assistant tells you he/she has trouble making ends meet on his/her salary.
   a. Let's take a look at your budget.
   b. With the number of hours I put in, I get less per hour than you.
   c. Your salary is rather low.
   d. I don't want to hear any more complaints from you.
   e. You feel you're not earning enough money.

8. An employee says that in spite of how others feel, she/he likes the job.
   a. Sure, sure, you just love your job.
   b. I can understand why a lot of people don't like it here.
   c. I don't like you gossiping about how others feel.
   d. You feel pleased here, even though others don't share your opinion.
   e. What do you think they dislike about working here?

9. A salesperson's performance has fallen off during the last two months.
   a. Things must be tough out there.

TABLE 3.1 (Continued)

b. You'd better bring those sales up, or else.
c. You seem troubled because your sales are off.
d. What's been the matter lately?
e. I don't think you've been trying very hard the last two months.

10. A supervisor tells you she/he has been having trouble with one of her/his workers.

a. Any decent supervisor could handle that problem by her/himself.
b. I guess his/her behavior really bothers you.
c. What have you done to try to motivate him/her?
d. I'll get a crying towel for you.
e. It isn't fair of him/her to do that to you.

Scoring

Circle the letters below that match the responses you circled. Then add up the columns to find your response style.

	U	CH	CR	S	A
1.	a	b	c	d	e
2.	e	a	b	c	d
3.	d	e	a	b	c
4.	c	d	e	a	b
5.	b	c	d	e	a
6.	a	b	c	d	e
7.	e	a	b	c	d
8.	d	e	a	b	c
9.	c	d	e	a	b
10.	b	c	d	e	a
COLUMN TOTALS	___	___	___	___	___

Interpretation

U is your tendency to give **understanding** responses. These are responses that summarize the content and feeling of what the speaker said. They are what we'll later discuss as "reflection."

CH is your tendency to give **challenging** remarks. These are responses

TABLE 3.1 (Continued)

	that ask for more information, or put the responsibility on the subordinate.
CR	is your tendency to give *critical* remarks. These are responses that judge or put down the subordinate—e.g., with sarcasm.
S	is your tendency to give *sympathetic* responses. These are remarks that focus solely on the subordinates' feelings, such as by agreeing, or criticizing a third person.
A	is your tendency to give *aggressive* responses. These are angry responses or ones that devalue the subordinate.

Reprinted by courtesy of Learning Dynamics, Inc., from "r-Dimension Leadership" program, Session II.

Most of us want our subordinates to like and admire us and at the same time achieve peak productivity and performance. But how do you achieve this goal? The key, as we said earlier, is to build trust between ourselves and our subordinates. In fact, this is our most important job as a manager.

Belief and Trust in Others

No matter how many techniques and skills you learn in this or any other book, you will not get very far without first learning to appreciate the abilities and potential of others. This is so important that if you use this principle *alone*, you can succeed with a variety of methods; but without it, you court failure no matter what approach you take.

No matter how much you know about techniques, your knowledge isn't worth much unless you know how much other people can *do*, given the right opportunities. So give them *your* confidence, your support, your trust. Encourage them to talk to you about their jobs, their ideas, and their problems. Seek out their ideas and use them, when you can constructively do so.

At one seminar, an older woman supervisor disagreed violently with this idea. Said she: "Oh, that all sounds fine and dandy if you're talking about ambitious, hard workers who are really motivated. But my people are all so lazy and indifferent, I wouldn't trust them to call the fire department if the building was burning down!"

Many managers—both men and women—feel that way. So first, let's examine the reason for a supervisor having lazy, indifferent employees. Those who have studied this problem agree that everything starts with *you—your* attitudes and *your* feelings about your subordinates.

One of the pioneers of the study of effective management was Douglas McGregor.[2] He described two basic types of management attitudes which he called Theory X and Theory Y.

McGregor's Theory X and Theory Y

Those whose management practices fall within McGregor's Theory X make certain assumptions about people:

1. People dislike work and will avoid it if they can.
2. People avoid challenge and responsibility.
3. Most of all, people look for security in jobs.
4. Because people dislike work and won't accept responsibility, they must be directed, controlled, coerced, or threatened to get them to do what they should.

Both the formal and informal leader styles are based on Theory X assumptions about people. Formal leaders manage through a "hard" approach—tight controls and threat of punishment—and the results are often decreased output, antagonism, resentment, and other types of backlash. Informal leaders, on the other hand, use a soft approach—a laissez-faire, "hands-off" style, with the object of trying to keep harmony in the organization. Here, the results are often a lack of direction, decreased output, and lazy, indifferent workers. These two styles are at opposite ends of the permissive/nonpermissive spectrum.

According to McGregor, Theory Y managers believe that

1. Work is as natural for people as play or rest. Depending on what it is, work can be satisfying or frustrating, and it will accordingly be done willingly or unwillingly.
2. People will work toward objectives to which they are committed.
3. Commitment to objectives relates to need satisfaction.
4. Under appropriate conditions, people not only accept responsibility, but seek it.
5. Typically, people have more ability than they use in the job.

[2]Douglas McGregor, *The Human Side of Enterprise* (New York: McGraw-Hill Book Co., 1960), pp. 133-34.

McGregor believed that Theory X assumptions about the nature of people are unrealistic. They become self-fulfilling prophecies. That is, when management believes that people inherently dislike and avoid work, people *will* come to dislike and avoid work. On the other hand, Theory Y managers believe in and trust their workers. This enables them to develop realistic strategies for leading others and to create a job climate in which motivation and morale are high. Obviously, those who believe in high achievement leadership subscribe to McGregor's Theory Y views.

In later chapters, we'll deal with the specific *people* skills for the high achievement style of management. In this chapter, we'll talk about the overall strategy of this style.

CREATING THE BEST
JOB CLIMATE FOR MOTIVATION

In the past twenty years, a vast body of research has been done on the problem of motivating workers.[3]

Human motives are internal drives that make people behave the way they do. We all have motives, like being recognized, getting ahead, having friends, providing for our families, and financial security. *Striving to meet motives* or aroused motivation, on the other hand, is a pattern of behavior designed to *achieve* our motives.

One person can't permanently arouse motivation in another person. But it is possible to create a specific environment or climate that will either nurture or discourage already existing motives.

What does this have to do with you as a manager? A great deal— because it is a major thesis in this book that the single most important influence on the job climate is the leadership style of the manager—you.

---

[3]Douglas McGregor, *The Human Side of Enterprise* (New York: McGraw-Hill Book Co., 1960), David C. McClelland, "Business Drive and National Achievement," *Harvard Business Review*, July/August, 1962, pp. 99–112; R.R. Blake and H.S. Monton, *The Managerial Guide* (Houston, Tex.: 1964) Gulf Publishing Co.,; John W. Atkinson, *Introduction to Motivation* (New York: D. Van Nostrand Co., 1964); John W. Atkinson and N. T. Feather, eds., *A Theory of Achievement Motivation* (New York: John Wiley & Sons, 1966); Chris Argyris, *Increasing Leadership Effectiveness* (New York: John Wiley & Sons, 1976); Chris Argyris, *Management and Organizational Development* (New York: McGraw-Hill Book Co., 1971); R.N. Horowitz, "Achievement Correlates and the Executive Role" (unpublished honors dissertation, Harvard University, 1961).

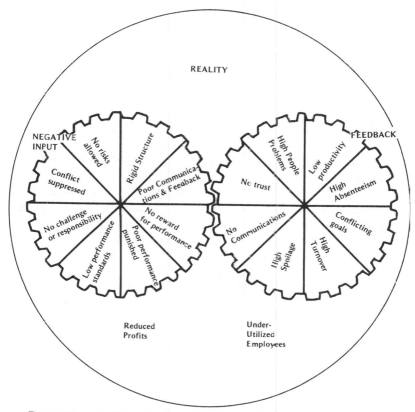

Figure 3.1   The Dynamic Leadership System-Negative Leadership Style

Yes, your style creates a climate that affects the behavior of your subordinates in important ways. Let's see how.

Negative Leadership Style

Figure 3.1 shows a version of the dynamic leadership system which illustrates a management style that creates *negative feedback*. The negative inputs are:

Figure 3.1 reprinted by courtesy of Learning Dynamics, Inc., from the "4 Dimension Leadership" program, 1975.

1. Rigid, structured petty rules and regulations
2. Poor communications and feedback
3. No rewards for performance
4. Low performance standards
5. No challenges or freedom to operate
6. No conflicts allowed
7. Punishment of poor performance
8. No risk-taking allowed

There is no real valuing of the human being with this style.

The feedback that negative input produces is predictable. People in this job climate are distrustful, defensive, unmotivated, frustrated, and bored. Productivity is low, absenteeism, and accident rates are high. And turnover is phenomenal. Employee reactions range all the way from "Some day 'I'll get out of this trap . . .'' "Let's vote for a union . . .'' to the most expensive reaction of all: "I quit."

Why do so many managers use a negative leadership style? I believe the primary cause is that managers *underestimate* the abilities of their employees. It's not that most managers overvalue themselves; instead they tend to *undervalue* the ability of others. That's *their* view of reality.

Positive Leadership Style

Now look at Figure 3.2. Here we see a positive leadership style, which creates positive feedback. The positive inputs result from these factors:

1. Rules are flexible and kept to a necessary minimum
2. Communications are open and feedback regular
3. There is a heavy emphasis on rewards
4. Performance standards are high
5. People are challenged and given freedom to operate
6. Conflicts are brought out into the open and resolved
7. Poor performance is *confronted*, not punished (there's a *big* difference)
8. Reasonable risk-taking is encouraged

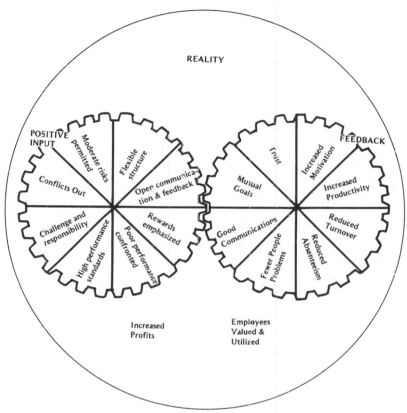

Figure 3.2   The Dynamic Leadership System-Positive Leadership Style

This is a climate in which the manager values human beings and understands the importance of human needs.

DIMENSIONS OF THE JOB CLIMATE

There are seven basic dimensions of the job climate created by individual leadership styles. And these dimensions, as you'll see, are closely interrelated. As a good manager, you need to be aware of these dimensions

Figure 3.2 reprinted by courtesy of Learning Dynamics, Inc., from the ''4 Dimension Leadership'' program, 1975.

in order to develop a leadership style conducive to maximum performance and satisfied workers.

Structure and Control

The first dimension of the job climate we'll examine is *structure*. How rigid or flexible are the rules and regulations? What are the avenues of communication between managers and subordinates? Are these avenues open or rigidly bound by formal rules? What limitations and rules are given to workers? Are they iron-clad, or is there some "give"? How are rules presented and enforced? How much information is available to workers? What constraints are placed on behavior? How strict are job definitions? In short, *how much control do managers exert?*

The degree of structure and control in any organization has a profound impact on the behavior of both the group as a whole and the individuals within it. A number of major studies by McGregor, Likert, Atkinson, Argyris, and others conclude that employee attendance records, safety records, on-the-job satisfaction, and length of employment are *directly* related to what we call "structure."[4]

Here's an example of the importance of structure in an organization. Some months ago, I had lunch with Janet, one of my former students. I greeted her and asked her how her big new job was going.

She replied: "Well, it's hard to say. I sent in what I thought was a great proposal to automate our credit checking procedures—three months ago. And would you believe it, I haven't heard anything. I did hear a rumor that the controller is blocking it, but I don't know why. I still don't know what's happening, and I'm pretty discouraged."

I asked: "Have you talked to the controller to see what the objections are?"

"Oh, you can't do that in *this* company. It's not like the good old days, at First Federal. We don't cross lines of authority—or step out of proper avenues of communications. I can only go through my immediate boss, and he's not much help. He says things like, 'These things take time,' and 'Be patient.' I don't think he knows any more than I do. It's really frustrating. And just between us, I'm giving serious thought to quitting."

[4]Ibid.

Well, she did quit. And another promising executive was lost . . . unnecessarily. The problems that were frustrating Janet are problems which any company—regardless of size—can avoid.

Coincidentally, not long ago, I was asked to make a training proposal to the company Janet had left. During a meeting with the company executives, the president complained, "I don't know what's happened to all the bright, enthusiastic young *idea* people we used to have. In the old days, I used to get a stream of ideas for improving things, or for new and better ways to solve problems. Now that we've branched out and become so organized, no one seems to come up with this sort of constructive help any more."

The vice-president added, "It's been worrying me, too. But you know, the other morning I spent three and a half hours just reading all our rules, regulations, manuals, and procedures for this, that, and the other thing. It occurred to me that maybe now we have so much emphasis on *how* we do things, we've stifled a lot of creativity and communication that came from our people."

This observation was really ironic—because Janet, before she quit, and her company's top executives were talking about the same problem. Too many rules and regulations; too many limitations on the job; too narrow avenues of communication. Too much emphasis on chain of command, too little feedback, too much control . . . in other words, *too much structure*.

An overstructured organization stifles personal incentive, creativity, and motivation—and it nourishes status-seeking, empire-building, and "politicking" behaviors. It is the most expensive problem that an organization can have. So, a major part of truly valuing those who work for you involves loosening up the structure.

How to Prevent Overstructuring

Personal Example. What can you do to prevent overstructuring? The first and most powerful method is through your *personal* example. This sounds simple, but don't underestimate its importance. If *your* door is closed, if *you* are hard to reach, if *you* are a remote, unreachable authoritarian—you can be sure this "climate" will go right down the line to your subordinates.

Begin by keeping your door open—literally and figuratively. Encourage your immediate subordinates to talk to you about ideas and problems. Take the time to discuss things—don't just reel off decisions. Of course this will cause interruptions and is time-consuming. However, as a *high achiever manager*, it is your job to work through people and *develop* their talents—not to control everything.

In addition to keeping your door open, get out there and see what's going on. Be visible, approachable, interested in people and their job problems. And while you're out there, keep your eyes open for these signs of an overstructured job climate:

1. Lack of communication between levels of administration—too much distance between the top and the bottom.

2. Poor team spirit and low individual morale. How busy and active are people in different departments? Do they seem cheerful and outgoing? One good test of morale is the condition of the lavatories. Take a look—are they littered? Cigarette butts ground out on the floor? Paper towels thrown helter-skelter? Graffiti on the walls?

3. Another sign of an overstructured job climate is a slow response to problems like outside competition. In live companies, ideas bubble up.

4. Still another sign of overstructuring is a heavy concern for status-seeking and empire-building. This signals that the emphasis is on power—not on achieving.

5. Finally, watch for a rigid chain-of-command syndrome. This is simply a device for protecting power—and it does not serve the company's needs for flexible avenues of communication.

Once you are back in your office, take positive steps to *reduce and prevent* an overstructured job climate.

Re-evaluation of policies.   Start first by re-evaluating your established policies and your "unwritten laws." Such policy re-evaluations can keep a company alive. And they are especially important in areas of rules and regulations. Some companies have many specific spelled-out rules and various unwritten laws and customs that have nothing to do with the reality of running a successful business.

For example, an organization in which there is a formal job climate may have a dress code like this: "All of our male sales personnel must be at least 6 feet tall, they must wear dark, conservative business suits, white shirts, knitted black ties, and short hair. Female sales personnel must wear skirts below the knees, no slacks, conservative jewelry and makeup, and high necklines."

An organization in which there is a high achievement climate might handle dress code this way: "We're pretty casual around here. We don't have strict dress codes. We expect that our employees will dress appropriately to the situation. We trust *them*, for example, to know that meetings with important clients involve wearing different clothes than those they'd wear at a departmental 'brainstorming session' or a company picnic."

An organization with a formal job climate might have rules like this: "All correspondence requires a pink copy, a yellow copy, a green copy, and a blue copy. Pink copies are to be put in a three-ring binder and submitted once a week to supervisors. Green copies are for the file . . ."

In a high achievement atmosphere, you might tell an employee this: "Correspondence gets prompt attention. Sometimes, if we have a knotty problem to answer by letter, we check with one or two others for an opinion before we mail it. Of course, if the letter is to be circulated, we know you'll be aware that a file copy and extra copies should be made, too."

Allow workers freedom to set individual goals.   In thinking about policy, remember that as a manager, your job is to *set* overall policies and goals in your unit or department. Then, for the best results, give your people the freedom to set individual goals and procedures. You can't be everywhere and control everything. If you are going to create a high achievement climate, controlling everything isn't your goal, anyway.

As you have probably noticed by now, the *structural* dimension of an organization has an important affect on all the other dimensions that create job climate. Now let's take a look at these other dimensions.

Individual Responsibility

The second dimension of the job climate that you as a manager can influence with your leadership style is that of *individual responsibility*. How much innovation is allowed? How much feedback on performance is given? What restrictions are there on individual accountability? How much participation is there in decision-making? How much *freedom* is there to operate?

Giving people real responsibility means that you are encouraging their desire to grow. This affects their loyalty, job satisfaction, mental health, and most importantly, their level of *performance*.[5] Of course, there are some people who run from responsibility. But increasing the personal responsibility of your workers is a way of showing that you value people. Furthermore, it nurtures their desire to achieve.

Of the three basic leadership styles (formal, informal, and high achievement), only the high achievement style emphasizes personal responsibility.

As was mentioned earlier, the primary reason managers fail is that they underestimate the ability of their subordinates. Such managers, under pressure, are likely to say things like: "My project is way behind schedule. I've got to have more people!" or "Cut back three people? It just isn't possible. We're shorthanded as it is!" or "I understand we need to increase production. And I'll do it if you'll get me the additional staff I need."

The fact is that generally, a great deal of talent within the organization may be unused. There are ways to increase productivity that utilize this knowledge. It is possible to fully use existing talent by means of two basic approaches: delegating and stretching.

Delegating.   There are many false ideas about delegating. Constructive delegating is *not*, as many think, a question of whether "you do it or I do it." It isn't letting someone else do the job while you sit back and judge how well it's being done, either. Nor is it doing the job together, with the other person acting as your assistant. What *is* good delegating?

Good delegating means giving the job to someone else to do, trusting that that person will do it right, while *you stay accountable* for what happens. You stay with it . . . keep your hand in. In other words, you manage. Here are some important steps in effective delegation adapted from William B. Given's *How to Manage People*:[6]

1. Discuss the job with your subordinate before asking him or her to go ahead. Talk over what you want done and what standards are important. Ask how well he or she understands what you want done. If you do discuss ways and means, be flexible. You can suggest new ways, but remember that each individual's natural way of working is usually the best way.

[5]R.N. Horowitz, "Achievement Correlates and the Executive Role" (unpublished honors dissertation, Harvard University, 1961).

[6]William B. Given, *How to Manage People* (Englewood Cliff, N.J.: Prentice-Hall, Inc., 1964), pp. 115–19.

2. Reach an understanding on which problems get reported back to you. You don't want to hear about every little difficulty. You do want to know about unexpected developments, bottlenecks, important disagreements with other departments, and any failure to meet schedule.

3. Set up a schedule for the project. Set deadlines for each member of the staff. Or, there may be a series of jobs to do before achieving the goals you set, such as purchasing certain materials in advance of a test, or getting accounting reports to different departments. Such a schedule helps you keep on top of what's going on—and automatically puts the heat on your subordinates to keep on schedule.

4. Get out there and see personally what's going on. How is your subordinate acting with his or her own people? How busy and productive is the staff? Remember, your personal interest in a project is one of the most important ways you can show you value your staff.

5. Ask for progress reports. These can be simple memoranda stating how things are going, or what changes are being planned—or they can be highly comprehensive, detailed analyses of the work in progress. Another kind of report is the kind your workers can put on their walls, using visual boards, charts, or graphs—that show everyone in the group how things are going.

6. Finally, have conferences now and then with your subordinate and his or her *group*, or with the heads of other departments who may be under your general supervision. Unless there is a special reason (such as a magazine requiring editorial content every second Monday), don't let these conferences become routine—or they will become time-consuming, unproductive, and may be regarded as interruptions and nuisances.

We'll say more about delegating later. For now let's look at the second major strategy for utilizing the talent of workers more effectively. This is called *stretching*.

Stretching.   Research shows that the majority of industrial employees, including managers, could operate from 25 to 50 percent more effectively than they do.[7] This is probably true because management typically reduces the work content of the job to a common level of mediocrity. But most people want challenge . . . want to improve . . . want to progress beyond their present assignments. How then, as a manager, can you help them *stretch?*

[7]Research conducted periodically by the American Management Associations.

You can encourage stretching by structuring the work to give each individual more challenge than he or she can easily handle. High achievement managers challenge others by setting appropriately high standards enlarging individual opportunities and by letting subordinates know what they have to do to progress.[8] Just as a football player needs to know how many yards he has to go for a first down, so does the supervisor need to know what to do to qualify as department head. If we know what we must do to advance, we're more likely to stretch ourselves—to take the necessary steps to get ahead.

Performance Standards

This brings us to the third dimension of the job climate: *performance standards*—for both individual employees and the organization as a whole. Of course, most thoughtful managers understand the importance of setting high standards. Why, then, are sloppy standards such a chronic problem in so many businesses today?

One vital reason is that too many managers settle for incompetent work. Although the importance of valuing people and their talents can't be overemphasized, a manager cannot neglect the importance of *performance and results*. This involves an attitude called "tough-mindedness." Just what is this tough-mindedness? Does it imply rigid control, an overstructured job atmosphere, disregard of people's needs and motivations? Or is tough-mindedness a positive quality in a manager—an ability to see into people's needs and capabilities, and to *stretch* them to do their best?

Tough-mindedness means keeping your subordinates on their toes by expecting them to do their best. One way to do this is by asking them challenging questions. This will ultimately improve the department's progress and at the same time improve the progress of the individual workers. For example, if a supervisor comes to you with a problem, how can you be tough-minded? Instead of giving him a solution, you could ask: "Well, Bill, what would you do if this were your division?"

If people know they're going to get questions like this, they'll spend a lot more time thinking about it before coming into your office. They will automatically focus on doing their best—giving you and the company their best efforts. And if they are spending more time thinking about solutions to problems, they are growing.

[8]Rensis Likert, *New Patterns of Management* (New York: McGraw-Hill Book Co., 1961), pp. 39–43, 119–39, 166–69.

Another part of tough-mindedness involves the honesty and feelings you provide in your feedback on performance. People need to know what's expected of them, the reasons for decisions and changes, and how they are progressing. But how do you provide feedback to subordinates who make mistakes, aren't performing well, or fail badly on something you've delegated to them? On this point I disagree with much of the published material on organizational development—most of which suggests that criticism is not a good method. I believe that people need to be confronted with criticism for poor performance—but gently! Confrontation of this sort *doesn't* involve blame, attack, or devaluation. Rather, it involves providing realistic, straightforward, constructive, honest feedback on workers' performance.

If your relationship with your subordinates is open and trusting, they will accept such criticism and see it as your way of helping them improve performance. And if criticism is offered in the right way, it can set the stage for subordinates to come right back to you with frank questions and sincere requests for help.

So, don't miss opportunities to honestly comment on subordinates' failures. Even though this isn't always easy to do, it is a necessary part of helping people to develop. This is one of your important responsibilities as a manager. When you confront a subordinate with criticism, emphasize ways to improve rather than dwelling on the failure. Don't say, "Why did you do this?" Instead, ask: "How can we avoid this again?" This will encourage good communication and provide the opportunity for you to help this person improve—to become a more competent and effective employee. Never forget that if you tolerate incompetence, incompetence is what you will get.

Rewards

Now let's look at the next dimension of job climate, which is closely related to the dimension of performance standards. This dimension involves rewards. Is high performance approved and rewarded? Is the reward system objective, specific, prompt, and performance-based? Are rewards just in money, or do they include feedback, praise, status rewards and promotion?

A high achieving job climate is one that emphasizes *rewards for excellent performance* rather than punishment for failure. This climate is much more likely to arouse a desire to achieve—and it also reduces the negative and destructive fear of failure. So it is wise to reward subordinates for their performance frequently and realistically. In doing so, keep in mind that salary increases and promotions are not the only rewards at your disposal. Recognition is a powerful reward. Verbal praise in private and public builds esteem. This means more than simply saying, "You're doing a good job." Be more specific—you can say, "You turn your work out with fewer errors than anyone I've ever had in this job. Keep up the good work. We'll both get ahead faster with performance like that!"

Some other ways to reward top performers are to consult them about changes you are considering—making it clear you are doing this because you think they are key people. Or, make them more visible to people higher up in the organization. For example, after a particularly well-done assignment, tell your superiors about it. You might even ask if one of them will write the subordinate an individual memo saying that you mentioned what a fine job he or she did.

Still other ways of rewarding include inviting subordinates to attend seminars. This gives them a break in routine *and* an opportunity to learn new skills. Or you can involve them in special projects, which may require some outside travel or research. You can give them more of your own time and informal coaching to develop their potential. Visiting their offices and desks instead of having them come to you is another device. In this way you give visible evidence of your special interest in high performers.

A word of caution on rewarding others: be certain that you tie your rewards to the high performance of your subordinates—or they may not understand that these signs of recognition are meant as rewards. And provide rewards as soon as possible after the high performance. An employee's diligence, innovation, and cooperation deserve attention. And a manager's commitment to a subordinate encourages top performance— far more than you may realize.

Feedback.   One of the most important ways to reward subordinates is through *feedback*, although feedback differs somewhat from classic reward systems. Rewards are related to approval, an important stimulation for achievement motivation. Feedback may or may not be related to approval, because it gives concrete measurement of how an individual or the group is doing. It can prove a person is right or wrong. However, people with a high need to achieve have a compelling interest to know how they are doing.

We've already discussed how to provide feedback to subordinates who make mistakes or otherwise fail in their responsibilities. But your feedback to those who work for you needs to be much broader and more consistent than simply dealing with poor performance. You need also to be ready to provide informative feedback on the job situation. There are four other areas of information that are important to remember in providing feedback. Be prepared to give the following additional types of feedback:

1. Information about how things are going, why things are being done, and especially regarding outstanding employee performance. This kind of information makes people feel part of things—and also goes a long way in preventing damaging rumors.

2. Information that announces and rewards excellent performance—of individuals and groups. This can be done with a simple "Thank you"—or with a notice on the bulletin board. It doesn't have to be expensive—just consistent.

3. Information that gives support, and encourages participation such as suggestions from employees.

4. Information that challenges. This can be done through setting high standards—and through supplying economic information, good or bad, and news about productivity, costs, competition, and other factors that affect subordinates' jobs.

Ways of Providing Feedback.   Through what channels do you provide feedback? There are dozens of ways.

Almost all companies, large and small, have some kind of formal communication program, ranging from face-to-face meetings, notices on bulletin boards, company booklets and newsletters, all the way to closed-circuit television messages. Of these, by far the most important method of providing feedback is face-to-face communication. Only with this type of communication can you immediately find out whether or not your message has been understood.

Face-to-face discussions are not always possible—but when they are, the focus should be on the work being done to achieve objectives, the problems that arise, and ways they can be solved. Remember, your purpose is not to attack or devalue. It's to solve a problem. So discuss it openly and get your subordinate's reaction. If he or she gets defensive, don't attack his/her excuses. Try to get feelings out into the open. Ask about feelings, then listen. Such discussions also permit you to immediately check on whether or not you've been understood. To do this, ask your worker to run through your instructions, or tell you his or her understanding of what you've said.

Always watch for nonverbal clues: facial expressions like raised eyebrows or frowns, a look of understanding or bewilderment. Remember too to use simple, direct language. Also, make sure you listen to the other person's responses. Pay attention to the words—as well as the feelings, attitudes, and values—your employee is communicating to you.

Warmth and Support

Another important dimension of the job climate is the degree of warmth and support that exists in the job situation. How much help and encouragement is given? Is the climate open, warm, and friendly? Do you show consideration for employees' feelings? How much respect do you give them? How much mutual trust exists?

Support, respect, and encouragement are important human needs that have to be satisfied. And mutual trust and consideration nurture loyalty, cooperation, job satisfaction, and a high level of performance. But use caution in this area—because it's common for managers to try so hard to create a warm, relaxed, easygoing, friendly climate that *doing the job* often becomes a secondary concern.

Field studies do not generally differentiate between support and warmth in organizational situations. However, taken together, there is a great deal of evidence that they have striking effects on motivated behavior. McGregor (1960) views employee-centered warmth and support as a necessary part of "Theory Y" management. Vroom (1964) calls it "consideration" and names it as a major determinant in job satisfaction. Halpin and Winer (1957) advocate supervisory behavior "of friendship, mutual trust, respect and warmth." Likert's (1961) ideal organization system is the creation of a "supportive atmosphere" . . . "with mutual trust and confidence."

The theory of achievement motivation leads me to believe that support and encouragement in the situation are more important than warmth and friendliness, in triggering motivation striving. When an individual is supported, encouraged, and valued, fear of failure is reduced and achievement-activity tends to increase. On the other hand, warmth and friendliness may reduce work-related anxieties, but there is no evidence that a happy-go-lucky environment will arouse achievement motivation.

Cooperation and Conflict

Another dimension of the job climate has to do with the degree of cooperation and conflict on the job. The high achievement climate has a lot of conflict, precisely because the people are focusing on getting the job done. And in doing so they often get in each other's way. So the way conflicts are handled is critical. Is conflict avoided entirely and cooperation stressed? Are conflicts usually settled by compromise? Or, instead of avoiding conflicts or compromising, are conflicts usually handled through confrontation—getting them out into the open?

To stress cooperation is healthy, of course. but it often becomes necessary to deal with conflict. How should this be done? Getting conflict out into the open through direct confrontation is the best way to increase the flow of information—both factual and emotional. More information helps clarify goals and provides feedback on performance. It brings choices for action and obstacles to goals into the open. So, confronting conflict rather than suppressing and/or avoiding it is the soundest management approach. Peace at any price through compromise is not your best course of action. Your real choice as a manager is *how* to handle conflict . . . not *if* you should handle conflict.

In Chapter 8 we will discuss some specific skills for handling conflicts effectively.

Opportunities for Risk-Taking

The final dimension of job climate involves opportunities provided employees for taking risks. Does the job climate discourage or encourage risk-taking? Are subordinates challenged to try new things? What degree of risk-taking do you allow? Some? None at all? A great deal?

People in business are always taking calculated risks. If they play it safe and refuse to try new things, they are likely to lose out. On the other hand, if they are too speculative or gamble too much, they may lose out, too. Therefore, the business climate that allows and encourages *moderate* risk-taking is dealing with *reality*. Allowing subordinates to set realistic goals and take moderate risks challenges them to do their best, gives them a feeling of involvement and pride in the organization, and makes the job exciting and fun for them.

Of course, success doesn't automatically follow risk-taking, but the successes far outweigh the failures. When capable people are challenged with the idea that success or failure is up to *them*, their self-esteem is usually positively affected. Given the freedom to act, people will generally do more and better thinking and more and better work. This is what produces high achievement conditions.

It is best for you as a high achievement manager to give subordinates freedom on jobs they can understand. And it's vital not to underestimate their ability. Even though they make some mistakes, they will gain experience in performing. The only way you can increase the number of achievers in your organization or unit is to give people the opportunity to take risks and to perform new kinds of work.

Also, it's important to give subordinates the freedom to fail. This doesn't mean to withhold your advice. You need to be available to help. But if you allow your people to think on their own, question established procedures, and experiment with new ideas without fear of failure, you will be helping them grow through risk-taking—and this growth will be good for them and for the company.

There is another important aspect in taking risks beyond betting on your people. This is to be willing to take risks yourself. Every successful entrepreneur knows this. However, too often, managers—especially women—are overcautious, refusing to take risks for fear of rocking the boat. Actually, more mistakes are made and more opportunities missed from fixed, inflexible opinions than from taking calculated risks. Overcaution is a menace to your chances of being successful—and if you do take calculated risks on people and on yourself, the percentages will be in your favor.

SUM-UP

In this chapter we have focused on the most effective leadership style within an organization, and on the strategies involved in operating as a high achieving manager. Throughout the chapter is the central principle of valuing others as human beings and of giving them full credit for their potential, as well as a chance to use it. This principle is the key to everything that follows in this book.

4
What Makes
People Tick

What makes people tick? What kinds of things do they like and dislike about their jobs? And how can this knowledge about people help you be the best possible high achieving manager? Here are a few comments from working people I've interviewed that may help you understand people better.

Question. What don't you like about your job?
Executive secretary:

Jobs are not big enough for people. It's not just the assembly line worker whose job is too small for his spirit, you know? A job like mine, if you really put your spirit into it, you would sabotage immediately. My boss will come in and say, "I know you're overloaded, but would you mind getting this done? It's urgent. I need it in three weeks." I can do it in two hours.

Editor:

It's so demeaning to be there and not be challenged. It's humiliation, because I feel I'm forced into doing something I would never do of my own free will—which is simply waste itself. I'm being had. Somebody has bought the right to you for eight hours a day. The manner in which they use you is completely at their discretion. You know what I mean?"

Bank teller:

We have a time clock. It's really terrible. You have a card that you put in the machine and it punches the time that you've arrived. If you get there after 8:45, they yell and they scream a lot and say, "Late!"

I've never felt you should be tied to something like a clock. My supervisor yells at me. He's about fifty, in a position that he doesn't really enjoy. You ask a question a lot of times, and you don't get the answer you need. Like he doesn't listen.

Computer programmer:

I know what I do is important, but nobody ever lets me know it. Sometimes I feel like the only friend I have around here is the computer, because the only part of me that anyone sees is the print-outs. Sometimes I even dream about pushing a few switches and erasing the whole business—that's how frustrated I get.

Now let's get the management side of the picture.

Question.   What do your people complain about most?
Sales manager:

Money. Dough, bread, gelt, mazuma, wampum, lettuce—that's what my people are always yelling about. It's what makes the world go around. Without it, none of them would do anything.

Personnel manager:

I don't know. With taxes so high these days, money doesn't mean so much any more. They can make more in fringe benefits, and Uncle Sam doesn't get a bite. Give them insurance, plenty of days off, long vacations, a pension, and that's what workers are asking for now.

Plant supervisor:

I've found that no matter how much you give people in salary or benefits, they're never satisfied. They want pleasant surroundings. A small investment in plants makes a big difference. The right colors, climate control, lighting, furniture, and music make them happy.

Research manager:

Working conditions don't mean anything. You can give workers everything, but they won't be content without the right leadership. Supervision is the key. A bad boss causes the most grumbling.

Plant manager:

My workers are unhappy being stuck in dead-end jobs. Advancement is the best thing in the world to cheer up employees. They like to feel they have responsibility . . . that they're somebody.

Area supervisor:

My workers say they get no recognition for a job well done. Workers in other companies get write-ups in the company paper, awards dinners, contests for secretary of the month. I think a small investment in a brass cup would pay large dividends in output.

Assembly-line supervisor:

What about the work itself? A lot of my people don't have any incentives. They get no internal satisfaction from a boring job. Conditions around here are perfect—but they still hate their jobs.

What really makes people tick? What motivates them to work hard? What causes problem behavior? When people ought to do something, why don't they? And why don't they strive to do their best?

BASIC HUMAN NEEDS

Most often it is because their basic human needs are not being met. Every one of us has the same basic needs which we strive to meet. If we don't succeed, we often try to fill them in different, even self-defeating ways—like being chronically late, making trouble, resisting changes, goofing off, failing on the job, drinking too much, and so forth.

Maslow's Hierarchy of Needs

Let's examine some of the basic human needs that motivate behavior. Figure 4.1 shows Abraham Maslow's familiar diagram of the hierarchy of needs.[1]

Maslow concluded that we are all motivated by the same basic needs. And as we satisfy lower needs in the hierarchy, we are motivated to meet higher ones.

Physical Needs.   First, there are the *basic physical needs* for such things as food, sex, clothing, shelter, activity, and rest. We go to great

---

[1]Abraham H. Maslow, "A Theory of Human Motivation," *Psychological Review* 50, 1943, pp: 370–396.

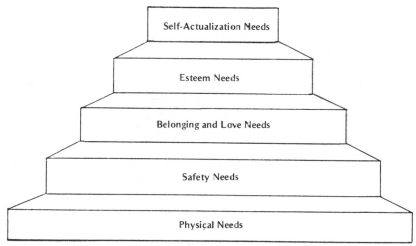

Figure 4.1   Abraham Maslow's Hierarchy of Needs

lengths to satisfy these needs, even if personal risk is involved. Once we have met these needs, we become concerned about the next level—the need for *physical safety*.

Safety Needs.   This means that we seek to avoid things that threaten our physical well-being, such as pain, sickness, noise, temperature extremes, and economic threat.

Need to Belong.   Maslow's third category concerns *our belonging needs*. Needs on this level include acceptance, friendship, and love. When people satisfy most of their need to belong, they may then seek to fulfill needs at the fourth level of hierarchy—esteem.

Need for Esteem.   Needs in this category are termed *ego needs*— they include prestige, status, respect, mastery, and freedom. Again, if our lower-level needs are in jeopardy, we will not be so concerned with meeting needs further up in the hierarchy.

Self-Actualization Needs.   Finally, highest in Maslow's hierarchy is the need for *self-actualization*. This highest human need involves realizing our full potential as human beings. Maslow concluded that once each need level is satisfied, it no longer acts as a primary motivator. But if the needs at one of the levels are not satisfied, it can lead to trouble.

Take the most basic level, for example. If people meet their physiological needs by getting enough food, activity, and rest, they will be alert and vigorous. If not, they will be tired and lethargic.

At the next level, people feel safe, relaxed, and secure when they have things like savings, insurance, and financial security. If these needs are not met, they may be anxious and nervous.

Likewise, when the social needs to belong are met, people are usually happy and well-adjusted. If not, they may become psychologically disturbed.

At level four are the so-called *ego needs*—involving self-esteem and the esteem of others. When these needs are met, people tend to be relaxed, outgoing, helpful, and kind. If esteem needs are not met, people may become defensive and demanding.

At the highest level, satisfaction of the self-actualization needs leads to growing, achieving, experimenting, and being creative. This makes people spontaneous, courageous, loving, and realistic. But if self-actualization needs are not met, this may lead to feelings of unhappiness or inadequacy.

Naturally, the strength of these needs varies in different people. And there is some overlap in the levels. For instance, we want to be safe at the same time that we want to be well-fed. But the important thing about the hierarchy is that once the needs at one level are satisifed, we tend to try to satisfy those needs at the next highest level.

Herzberg's Research on Needs

Frederick Herzberg carried out studies to test Maslow's theories.[2] He approached over 1,000 workers in different walks of life and asked them how they felt about their jobs. Specifically, he wanted to know what made workers feel good "satisfiers" and what made them feel bad "dissatisfiers." He asked them to think back to when they became significantly more or less satisfied with their job, and what had changed to make them feel that way. Before you read the results of Herzberg's studies, try the following exercise.

[2]F. Herzberg, B. Mausner and B. A. Snyderman, *The Motivation to Work* (New York: John Wiley & Sons, 1957); F. Herzberg, *Work and the Nature of Man* (New York: World Publishing Co., 1966).

Exercise

Look at Table 4.1. Write down what satisfies and dissatisfies you in your job.

Herzberg's research confirmed Maslow's theory. The things with which workers were most dissatisfied involved needs low on the hierarchy: company policy, working conditions, supervision, salary, etc. He referred to these factors as "hygienic"—if they remained unsatisfied, the worker felt bad. But they were not motivating by themselves if they were adequately fulfilled.

TABLE 4.1
Satisfiers and Dissatisfiers

Think back to a time when you felt extraordinarily good about your job. What changed to make you feel that way? Do the same thing for a time when you felt exceptionally bad.

FACTOR	GOOD	BAD
1. Achievement	_____	_____
2. Recognition	_____	_____
3. Responsibility	_____	_____
4. The work itself	_____	_____
5. Advancement	_____	_____
6. Possibility of growth	_____	_____
7. Company policy and administration	_____	_____
8. Working conditions	_____	_____
9. Salary and fringe benefits	_____	_____
10. Interpersonal relations	_____	_____
11. Status	_____	_____
12. Security	_____	_____
13. Supervision	_____	_____

Reprinted by courtesy of Learning Dynamics, Inc.

*One survey found that people are satisfied by factors in this order: (1) achievement, (2) recognition, (3) the work itself, (4) responsibility, (5) advancement, (6) salary, and (7) growth

They are dissatisfied by these (1) company policy, (2) supervision, (3) interpersonal relationships, (4) working conditions, (5) salary, (6) status, and (7) security.

In Herzberg's study, the *positive motivators*—or the satisfiers—mostly concerned the fulfillment of higher needs: for achievement, recognition, responsibility, the challenge of work itself, and the possibility of growth. These results usually held true no matter who was questioned—men or women, Americans or Europeans, executives or service workers.

Herzberg concluded that "the hygienic factors (dissatisfiers), like salary and working conditions, act like heroin. It takes more and more to produce less and less effort."

The "Dissatisfiers."   Let's examine each of these "dissatisfiers" briefly, specifically in relation to you as a manager.

First, there's money. Once you have workers on board, the dollar has little power to keep them interested. This is first, because it only comes once a week at most; and second, because to be effective, rewards need to come immediately after and be tied specifically to high-level performance.

Next, there's fringe benefits and working conditions. These are as important as salary in *attracting* employees, but like cash, they don't motivate as strongly once a person is hired. Vacations, holidays, pension plans, and health benefits help meet needs at the lower level of Maslow's hierarchy. But once these needs are met, they no longer have such a strong motivational force.

The Hawthorne Experiment

The pioneering study on working conditions was done in the 1930's and 40's at Western Electric's Hawthorne Plant.[3] Psychologists choose some assemblers, and put them in a room to test changes in lighting and hours. Increases in illumination and the number of rest pauses raised output, but so did *decreases*. It seemed that no matter what the experimenters did, *productivity went up*. The psychologists concluded that the assemblers' sense of importance, because they were being studied, and their compatibility in the group, led to increased output. The results of the Hawthorne Experiment shook the world of industrial psychology. Until then, researchers had believed that *external* factors—such as money, benefits, and working conditions—were the primary employee motivators. This experiment showed that human beings are motivated by *internal* factors.

The last "dissatisfier" concerns supervision. People need to have self-esteem and the respect and esteem of others. Managers can help employees satisfy these needs through open, two-way communications, by

[3]Fritz J. Roethlisberger, *Management and Morale* (Cambridge, Ma.: Harvard University Press, 1941).

avoiding petty rules and regulations, and by rewarding and valuing their workers. Few things demoralize workers as much as petty rules—such as needless restrictions on restroom trips, limitations on talking, unrealistic dress codes, arbitrary rules that have little to do with productivity. And almost nothing enrages employees as much as having managers criticize them in front of their colleagues—this is especially damaging to their self-esteem.

The Satisfiers. Let's take a look at the positive side. What are the factors that can make workers feel good about their jobs, and strive to produce? Factors like *advancement, responsibility, recognition,* and *the work itself.*

Advancement gives workers a boost. It also changes their self-image. If they *see* themselves as a valuable member of the team, they tend to *act* that way.

Responsibility goes hand-in-hand with advancement. However, you can increase the *scope* of someone's job without changing the title. As we saw in the last chapter, McGregor's Theory Y proposes that people naturally enjoy work, will work willingly toward objectives to which they are committed, and, under certain conditions not only want responsibility but seek it. Managers who agree with this idea give workers maximum freedom and responsibility to satisfy their needs while meeting the organization's goals. They consult workers before making decisions, and let workers decide many procedures for themselves. But a word of caution from management consultant David Sirota:

> Enrich a worker's job by giving him or her more responsibility, broader functions, more tasks, more variety. But if the worker's pay is either inadequate to begin with, or extra compensation doesn't come with extra work, the worker will feel she or he is being cheated and react accordingly.[4]

Recognition is important, too. Employees need to have others know that they have done well. Some companies have come up with novel techniques for showing recognition. There are material rewards like trips, TV sets, and trading stamps, given with public ceremony for outstanding performance. And there are nonmaterial ways of rewarding good performance—for example, mention in company publications, award of certificates, acknowledgment at dinners, and so forth.

[4]David Sirota, Boardroom Reports.

Finally, workers are motivated by a sense of *achievement*, a satisfaction they get from the work itself. Some work is inherently interesting, and sufficient to keep the worker going. For other work, what motivates is the end product, the results—finishing the job. Human beings seem to have an inner drive for mastery, a need to be competent. Most people want to have some effect on the world. When they accomplish something difficult, they feel good about it and this sparks them to seek more achievement.

If we can see that all people have these basic needs, it is easier to understand what makes them tick. Problem behavior usually results from an attempt to meet these needs. When people can't meet needs in direct ways, they try to meet them in indirect—and often self-defeating—ways. Let's examine some reasons for people behaving in self-defeating ways.

SELF-DEFEATING BEHAVIOR

Eric Berne, the founder of Transactional Analysis, has provided many insights into the reasons so many people have trouble coping effectively.[5] He believed the greatest problems came from what he calls *life scripts*. Let's see how negative life scripts develop.

Very early in life, we all make some very important decisions. These decisions have to do with our own self-concept and with our concept of other people and the world in which we lived. From these decisions, we develop our life script and also select our life's role.

Here are some of the kinds of decisions people make about themselves:

- I'm smart.
- I'm stupid.
- I'm capable.
- I can't do anything right.
- I'm an achiever.
- I'm a failure.
- I'm a happy, outgoing person.

[5]Eric Berne, *What Do You Say After You Say Hello?* (New York: Grove Press, 1972).

- Nobody likes me.
- Everybody will give me what I want.
- People are out to get me.
- Everybody loves me.

Roots of Life Scripts

All of these decisions have their roots in the messages we receive as children from our parents. These messages may give us a fairly realistic idea about ourselves, our talents, and how to get along in society. Or they may give us unrealistic, distorted, or even destructive ideas about ourselves.

From these decisions, all of us learn to play basic roles (e.g., persecutors, victims, or rescuers) and, as adults, we unknowingly seek out others with whom to play out complementary scripts.

This "scripting" first occurs nonverbally. Infants begin to receive messages about themselves and their worth through their early experiences of being touched or ignored by others. Later, they see facial expressions and hear the tone of voice used with them. Babies who are cuddled, talked to, and smiled at affectionately receive dramatically different messages about their worth than babies who are handled with fear, anxiety, indifference, or resentment.

Later, parents put script messages into words. For example:

- You're a wonderful son.
- Why couldn't you have been a boy?
- You'll never make it as an engineer—you're too slow in math.
- The Lord helps those who help themselves.
- Don't let the boys know you're smart, honey—it will scare them away.
- Well, our family has always had a black sheep—and you're it!

The problem with these messages is that even if they are unrealistic or even destructive, as adults we feel compelled to follow them. Why? So far, we do not have a complete understanding of this aspect of our personality. We only know that these messages, received very early, are likely to remain the most powerful influence in our lives; they are like commands we believe we must obey. In Berne's words,

Nearly all human activity is programmed by an ongoing script dating from early childhood, so that the feeling of autonomy is an illusion—an illusion which is the greatest affliction of the human race, because it makes awareness, honesty, creativity, and intimacy possible only for a few fortunate individuals. For the rest of humanity, other people are seen mainly as objects to be manipulated. They must be invited, persuaded, seduced, bribed, or forced into playing the proper roles to reinforce the protagonist positions and fulfill his script. And his preoccupation with these efforts keeps him from torquing in with the real world and his own possibilities in it.[6]

Every person is *born* a unique, free individual with particular capacities and potentials to develop, express, and experience. But too many of us give up this freedom, deny reality, and spend our time manipulating others to join the cast of characters for our life script.

Most parental messages are a mixture of constructive, destructive, and neutral elements. Unfortunately, however, some parents—because of their own problems—send messages that are *totally* destructive. For example:

- We'd be better off without you.
- You're too stupid and lazy to get anywhere.
- You're so scrawny, you'll never be a man.
- You poor little helpless thing, let me do that for you.
- Get lost!
- If anyone gets in your way, destroy them.

Later in life these destructive messages become unthinkingly accepted by us as part of reality. As such, they can only cause problems and unhappiness that range all the way from mild—rarely interfering with the ability to operate—to extremely serious—to the extent that people can't function.

Here are a few examples of life scripts:

Michael, as a youngster, received messages to obey the rules and perform well according to his parents' values. Now his major interest in life is doing a good job. When he isn't working, he is either planning his next move or resting up for a new onslaught. As a manager, he operates according to this script. People receive little

[6]Ibid.

attention—his focus is on his work. He places great stress on rules and regulations, and is highly critical of his subordinates if they break the rules or don't perform up to his standards. Since he's highly goal-oriented, he sets the goals and makes all the decisions. When problems arise, he feels he must suppress them. His message to subordinates is, "Follow the rules, obey the regulations, do your work, and everything will be fine." He is a rigid authoritarian. The problem is, no one likes to work for him, so they punish him with lateness, absenteeism, sloppy work, or by quitting. His script hasn't prepared him to find a way out of this situation. Rather, it has prepared him to stick to his guns, to try harder, and to demand more and more of his subordinates until he eventually either gets fired or gets kicked upstairs.

Here's another example:

The message Harriet received as a child was to be nice to other people so they would like her . . . and if she couldn't figure out how to be nice, she should at least not annoy others. So her script calls for avoiding pressure, controversy, or other disruptive activity. She never pushes people. She goes out of her way to do things for them. She tries to make everyone happy. The trouble is, she can never get people to work hard for her. People use her, take advantage of her generosity, and generally walk all over her.

It is sad that so many of us blindly follow unhappy life scripts. Eric Berne, in his book *What Do You Say After You Say Hello?*, expressed it this way:

How is it that the members of the human race, with all their accumulated wisdom, self-awareness, and desire for truth and self, can permit themselves to remain in such a mechanical situation, with its pathos and self-deception? Scripts are only possible because people don't know what they are doing to themselves and to others. But there are also certain remedies which can be applied.[7]

The Manager Helping Others to Grow

Of course, each of us is responsible for ourself; that responsibility includes understanding our life script—and getting rid of it. But even as a manager, you can help your subordinates with problems—first, by following the rules of valuing others (Table 4.2). Next, you can help by using a

[7]Ibid., pp. 244–245.

leadership style that creates a climate for achievement. Finally, you can help by employing the specific human relations skills you are learning in this book.

TABLE 4.2
Rules for Valuing Others

1. Pay attention and really listen to others—what they say, and the feelings they express.
2. Don't make assumptions about how others think or feel, or how they will react. You can't get inside anyone's head and crystal-ball gazing is for gypsies.
3. Sarcasm and kidding is dirty fighting.
4. Don't be destructively generous. Let others exercise their right to be responsible for themselves.
5. Try to send harmonious messages to avoid confusing others.
6. Disagree with or confront unrealistic or manipulative behavior, but don't attack others as humans.
7. Don't label others—as dumb, coward, lazy, childish—or don't make sweeping judgments about feelings, especially about whether the feelings are real or important or "morally" right or wrong.
8. Don't play manipulative games. Be honest, direct, open, and specific. And don't mind-rape. That is, don't correct others' statements about how they feel, or don't tell them how they "should" feel.
9. Be careful of how you use questions. They are a demanding, controlling form of communication, especially the "WHY?" or "WHY NOT?" question . . . which usually implies your disapproval.
10. Be tentative—don't state your opinions as facts, avoid preaching words, don't exaggerate or bulldoze others. Give them room to move.
11. When you have differences, be willing to mediate any differences and work out contracts. And when you do fight, *fight fair*.

Reprinted by courtesy of Learning Dynamics, Inc.

This adds up to getting involved and showing problem people you care about them first as human beings . . . that you accept them, despite their problems. This will build trust and show them you value their basic worth as human beings. Furthermore, valuing people rewards them; thus, when you value others, you strengthen their positive behavior. Abraham Maslow believed that respect is a powerful tool—one that anyone can use with "problem people." He said: "Every person who is kind, helpful, decent, psychologically democratic, affectionate and warm, is a psychotherapeutic force, even though a small one."

Respecting Workers

Exercise

Do you respect the people you manage? To find out, ask yourself the following questions:

1. Do I trust the capacities of the group, and of the individuals in the group, to meet the problems with which we are faced? Or do I basically trust only myself?
2. Do I free the group for creative discussions by being willing to understand, accept, and respect *all* attitudes? Or do I find myself trying subtly to manipulate group discussion so that it comes out my way?
3. Do I, as manager, participate by honest expression of my own attitudes, but without trying to control the attitudes of others? Do I rely upon basic attitudes for motivation? Or do I think surface procedures motivate behavior? Do I trust the individual to do his or her job? When tensions occur, do I try to make it possible for them to be brought out into the open?

If you can answer these questions "yes," you are on the right road. By showing subordinates that you respect them, you reduce their anxiety. They will feel less threatened by your behavior. This, in turn, increases their trust in you.

Examining Workers' Behavior

Once you have established a trusting relationship with any of your workers who have problems, begin to examine their behavior. Even though you accept them as human beings, you don't have to accept their unrealistic behaviors. Discuss problems openly, and try to get workers to examine their actions so they can see how unrealistic they are.

Confront subordinates who fail, make serious mistakes, or who behave in problem ways. As we've said, confronting isn't attacking. Confronting means that you point out their problems constructively. Here's an example: "Don, we set the completion date of this Acme presentation for ten days ago. You haven't told me about anything unexpected that's come up. What's happened?"

Or to someone who is engaged in self-defeating behavior such as frequent absenteeism: "You say you enjoy your work, and when you're here you do a good job. The trouble is, you're often not here, and it's creating problems with the rest of the staff. What's the reason? Maybe we can work it out."

Remember, your goal is not to make problem people feel better. Facing reality is sometimes painful. However, you as a manager need to look at long-run results rather than trying to gratify immediate desires to make others feel good. If, over the long term, you can help others change unrealistic, self-defeating behavior, you are doing them an immeasurable service. And, if you *can't* get them to change, it is well you know this so you can decide realistically whether they'd be better off in some other company.

Put Tasks on a Personal Basis

Another way of valuing people is to put all tasks on a personal basis. Involve yourself. Instead of saying: "You should be at your desk at 8:30 sharp, and no excuses," say instead: "I'd really appreciate it if you'd be at your desk on time." This will increase your personal involvement with your subordinates.

Take an Interest in Workers' Lives

Finally, you can show you value others by taking an interest in their personal lives. This may not seem important to you, but it is a powerful technique in showing others you care about them. Now and then, talk to them about topics not related to the job—such as their personal development, their children, their spouse, or their hobbies.

PERSONALITY NEEDS

Now, let's examine another area of needs human beings have: personality needs.

The theory of personality needs was suggested by Henry Murray of Harvard.[8] He had people make up stories about a series of pictures (such as

[8]H. A. Murray, *Explorations in Personality* (New York: John Wiley & Sons, 1938).

of an older and younger man). He found that people revealed their own subconscious motivations through their stories. From the results of this experiment, Murray developed a list of twenty personality needs—such as achievement, aggression, dominance, loyalty, and order—which people seek to meet through their behavior.

Three of these personality needs seem to be most important to worker motivation: the needs for achievement, dominance, and affiliation.[9] So let's examine ways in which you can identify these personality needs in order to be of most help to those you manage.

Achievement Needs

People who have a high need to achieve might sound like this:

I like to do difficult things. Jobs that are too easy bore me. I get real satisfaction from mastering something hard.

I'm not afraid to take risks when I'm in control, but I don't like to take wild chances, or depend too much on luck. If I put my money on something, I want to have a say in the outcome.

I want to know how I'm doing. If I make a mistake, I want to know about it. But when I do something right, I need to learn about that, too.

David McClelland of Harvard and others have conducted numerous studies showing that people who have a need for achievement actually do accomplish more.

If a job requires taking risks, overcoming obstacles, assuming responsibility, receiving feedback, and using freedom, it is an achievement task. Jobs in which workers can set their own standards and get rewarded for high performance are best filled by people with a high need for achievement. These are jobs like business executives, salespeople, consultants, fund-raisers, and engineers.

Affiliation Needs

People high in the need for affiliation sound like this:

I couldn't work alone—it would drive me crazy. I need a lot of friendly people around me to be able to get my job done.

[9]See also Douglas McGregor, *The Human Side of Enterprise* (New York: McGraw-Hill Book Co., 1960).

It's important to me to be liked. I believe in expressing positive feelings toward others, and I hope they'll let me know how they feel.

I enjoy helping others. When someone has a problem, I like to be the one they seek for advice.

The affiliation need is not related to achievement; a person with a need for affiliation may achieve a lot or a little, depending on other factors.

The need for affiliation is valuable in jobs that require friendly interaction. Positions that offer the opportunity to help others and to work in groups are good for people with this need. Appropriate occupations are teaching, nursing, counseling, coordinating, and research.

People voted "most likely to succeed" by their classmates are likely to be high in need for affiliation, rather than achievement. On a tough job, they would rather work with a friend than an expert, while people high in the need for achievement feel just the opposite.

Dominance Needs

People high in the need for dominance sound like this:

I've got to be my own boss. I can't stand taking orders from anyone else.

I stick up for what I believe, no matter what anyone else thinks. If this causes an argument now and them—well, I don't mind.

I don't have time to sit around discussing feelings. I've got responsibility, and I'll make the decisions, no matter whose toes get stepped on. I don't want anyone to think I'm indecisive.

As with affiliation needs, a high need for dominance does not in itself guarantee success. Success depends on the job, and on what other skills such people have.

High dominance needs are useful in rigid, hierarchical organizations. The military, teaching, politics, top management, law, and police work are some areas in which people with dominance/power needs tend to do well.

Is there any *best* type of personality need (in terms of doing a job well)?

Ideally, a person who has a high need in all three of these areas would be a high achieving worker. But this would be a rare person indeed.

For example, people who have a high need for dominance are apt to be so concerned with status and power that they fail to establish the climate most needed for achievement. They want to dominate everyone else, but few subordinates work well under such conditions. When power is an end in itself, little else gets done; indeed, those whose need for dominance is not tempered by other needs are unlikely to succeed in gaining power.

Those high only in the need for achievement may not attain positions in which they *can* achieve unless they have some power. If they do, they must be able to give orders to successfully delegate work to subordinates. If they do not have the human relations skills to work through others, their achievement will be limited, so some affiliation needs are necessary.

And a need for affiliation by itself is not enough. People who have an extremely high affiliation need will probably not achieve very much. If they have little need for achievement, they may not care if anything gets done beyond developing good, friendly relations with others. If they have little need for dominance, they will find it hard to supervise or criticize anybody else.

Since few people are high in all three of these personality needs, it is probably best to look for workers who are moderate in two needs and high in the third, depending on the job. When people are in the right jobs, their needs are met and they are more likely to succeed.

In one leadership seminar, a company president said, "It sounds like I've got all the right people in the wrong jobs. My salespeople seem to be high in the need for power, my managers seem to be high in the need for affiliation. What can I do? I can't fire them and start all over again, and it costs too much to shuffle personnel around and retrain them for the right positions. Is it possible to change people's needs?

Probably not; personality needs seem to be pretty fixed, from early in a person's life. However, people's existing motivations can be nurtured or discouraged by the organizational climate. It takes recognition, advancement, responsibility, valuing, and the work itself to get employees to strive to do their best.

Many managers say, "I don't have time to deal with the needs, motives, personalities, and development of my subordinates."

I say that a manager doesn't have the time *not* to. Why do you think you spend so much of your time on problems now? Because either your problems are growing more critical or you have neglected dealing with them adequately in the past. In either case, matters will only get worse if you put them off. Taking a little time now to build your subordinate's self-esteem and respect will save you a lot of time later. And it is *your job*—one of your *biggest* jobs—to develop the abilities of workers and supervisors reporting to you.

As was mentioned earlier, research shows that the majority of workers and managers could operate from 25 to 50 percent more effectively. If your company has no worries about competition or profit, then this situation need not concern you too much. But if your organization could use extra power and effectiveness, this is a strong argument for developing the abilities of those who work for you.

Most good people *want* to improve and are not content to remain at the same level indefinitely. So you do not help your company or your people by showing little interest in their development. In fact, your apathy and disinterest can generate more problems—of bitterness and resentment.

Too many good middle managers get bogged down in mediocre jobs because they haven't developed the abilities of their subordinates. *The best way to get ahead is to develop and promote the people who work for you.* Therefore, you really can't use time more productively than by helping your subordinates become more effective.

SUM-UP

In closing the chapter, I want to stress that meeting human needs leads to operating a profitable, growing company. It doesn't mean tolerating incompetence or half-hearted effort—or sacrificing your own best interests. Learning to lead others effectively really serves the best interests of the company—by maximizing your return on investment, in both productivity and increased motivation.

Is it worth the effort? Try answering these questions, suggested by Ray Killian in *Human Resource Management*:[10]

> What kinds of changes and results would occur if every employee in the company put forth his or her absolute best effort?

[10]Ray Killian *Human Resource Management: An ROI Approach (Return on Investment)* (New York: Amacom, 1976), pp. 126–27.

Suppose every employee worked like the track star does to win the race and strained as hard to be first to break the ribbon.

Suppose employees had the same interest and got the same satisfaction from their jobs as they do from hobbies and recreation.''

If this level of effort and commitment could be sustained, companies—and the world—would never be the same again.

5

Barriers
to
Communication

Communication has been discussed, written about, trained around, and chosen by management as the theme for conventions perhaps more than any other subject. And still it is the one skill that has achieved the least progress or result. Today our business environment is one of computers, visual aids, duplicating machines, audio and visual novelties, canned programs, electronic linkups, and an endless variety of communications tools. But, in the final analysis, communication is most importantly a one-to-one relationship.[1]

Here are a few examples illustrating communication problems:

A boss says angrily: "Of *course* you're doing a good job! Do I have to keep telling you?"

A fellow worker says: "There you go, making that same stupid mistake again—ha-ha!"

A subordinate asks: "Do you mind if I ask you something?"

Your supervisor says: "What do you mean, you're sick? You look OK to me."

A salesman says: "Well, I just *assumed* you wouldn't mind my using your office for a little while."

Your boss says: "I'm your supervisor!"

Your broker says: "It's smart to buy that stock at 30."

A great many of us send and receive messages like these all the time.

[1]Roy Killian, *Human Resource Management: An ROI Approach* (Return on Investment) (New York: American Management Assn., Inc., 1976).

Yet each one of these messages is an example of different types of barriers to effective, open, honest communication.

They illustrate problems like mixed messages, hidden assumptions, put downs, hidden aggression, and the like. And because such messages confuse or threaten the other person and put that person on the defensive, they are devaluing and they block effective communication.

BARRIERS TO COMMUNICATION

Let's examine these barriers.

A boss says angrily: "Of *course* you're doing a good job!"

The Mixed Message

This is an example of a mixed message. That is, the boss is saying *one* thing with words and *quite another* with tone of voice. The words are meaningless in this case. The real message is anger. But suppose he says it sincerely: "Of course you're doing a good job."

Now the *words* and the *tone of voice* communicate that the boss values you. Words and tone are matched instead of *mixed*. When you send mixed messages to others, you confuse them if you communicate two things at once. Often we send such messages when we are tense, preoccupied, busy, or pressured for time. Here are some more examples of mixed messages.

Someone says in a bored tone of voice: "Sure I'll be happy to listen to your presentation."

Or you ask a friend how she is and she answers nervously: "Oh, I'm fine—everything's just great. Couldn't be better, in fact."

Or a fellow worker says sarcastically: "Oh, I'm sooooo sorry you didn't get the promotion. Better luck next time."

One important goal in communications is harmony, which means that *what* you say is *what* you intend. There is a fit between the content of the message and the way you say it. The feelings involved in the process come out in your behavior. This includes tone, pitch, rate of speech, facial expression, and body language. If you say one thing with your words and another with your voice or behavior, your listeners are apt to become confused; or perhaps they'll only respond to one and not notice the other. Mixed messages damage your credibility.

Mixed messages confuse others. If people aren't sure which message to believe, chances are they won't believe either—and this is a barrier to effective communication.

What if people send mixed messages to you? How should you handle such messages?

First, the true message is almost always expressed by the *feeling* being communicated—the message being sent by tone of voice, gestures, and body language. Depending on the situation, you can ignore the content and just keep the feeling message as a useful piece of information about the person who sent it. Or you can gently confront the sender with something like: "You say you're sorry, but you honestly don't sound that way." Or "You say you're pretty enthusiastic, but I get the feeling that *something* is worrying you."

Exercise

Many studies have shown that as much as 85 percent of communication occurs through tone of voice, gestures, and body language![2] Tables 5.1 and 5.2 offer an experiment you can do with a partner to illustrate this. The content of both of these exercises is the same, but the feelings being communicated are totally different.

The Sarcastic Message

A fellow worker says: "There you go, making that same stupid mistake again—ha-ha!"

The "kidding" message is one of the most confusing and painful messages there is. Such messages are not supposed to be funny—they are meant to tease, confuse, put down, or devalue. They provide a safe,

[2]L. Sperry and L. W. Hess, *Contract Counseling* (Reading, Ma.: Addison Wesley, 1974), p. 68.

phony, cowardly cover for aggression. Such a message makes the kidder the wise and knowing one and his or her victim a stupid fool. People who are bullies or who feel inadequate often use kidding to ridicule or embarrass others without having to take responsibility for their true feelings.

Here's a typical exchange:

- You mean you don't know how to fill out a simple requisition? ha-ha.''
- Maybe I should stop asking you for help . . . so I don't bother you.''
- "Hey, what's the matter? Can't you take a joke? I was only *kidding*.''

TABLE 5.1
Content vs. Tone Dialogue No. 1

Read this with a partner—you take one role, your partner the other. Follow the instructions for tone and feeling as you read each line.

Tone	Dialogue
Confident	Sup: You sent for me, sir?
Proudly. (In the last sentence bear down on "*That's*.")	Chief: Yes—take another look at this project Smith completed. *That's* a report!
Also with pride.	Sup: Well, boss, you know the kind of people I have in my department. That's the kind of work they turn out.
Complimentary. (You are going to make sure he takes some credit.)	Chief: Don't be modest. Surely you had a share in this.
Modestly. (You don't want to take any glory away from Smith.)	Sup: Well, I reviewed it, of course. But with my load I have to rely on the man. Basically, it's Smith's product.
Jokingly. (You know he has done a lot to develop Smith.)	Chief: Now, now. You're not going to get out of it that easily.
Still modest. (But your arm has been twisted, and you're ready to admit you're pretty good.)	Sup: Well, if you say so, J.B., I suppose. I must admit to some share in the project.
Hopefully.	Chief: The question is, what about Smith? Can we continue to expect work like this?
Happy. (First sentence.)	Sup: Yes sir, we can. (Recalls

TABLE 5.1 (Continued)

Tone	Dialogue
Regretful. (Second sentence.)	something.) But Smith is being transferred.
With disappointment.	CHIEF: Oh no! I'll be sorry to see him go.
Regretfully. (How will you replace him?)	SUP: Yes. We're going to miss that boy around here!

From the Veteran's Administration Office of Personnel.

TABLE 5.2
Content vs. Tone Dialogue No. 2

Repeat the reading but this time read the lines with the new set of instructions for tone and feeling.

Tone	Dialogue
Fearful.	SUP: You sent for me, sir?
Sneer. (Make last sentence a question emphasizing word "Report?")	CHIEF: Yes, take another look at this project Smith completed. That's a report!
Apologetic. (A "what-can-you-expect" tone.)	SUP: Well, boss, you know the kind of people I have in my department. That's the kind of work they turn out.
Sarcastic. (You're not going to let him get away with it.)	CHIEF: Don't be modest. Surely you had a share in this.
Dodge. (If someone is going to be blamed, let it be Smith!)	SUP: Well, I reviewed it, of course. But with my load I have to rely on the man. Basically, it's Smith's product.
Still sarcastic. (You're not going to let him weasel out of this one!)	CHIEF: Now, now. You're not going to get out of it that easily.
Reluctantly. (Better yield, or you will be the target instead of Smith.)	SUP: Well, if you say so, J.B., I suppose I must admit to some share in the project.
Disgustedly. (Point to report with expression of distaste.)	CHIEF: The question is, what about Smith? Can we continue to expect work like this?
Regretful. (First sentence.) Happy. (Second sentence.)	SUP: Yes sir, we can. (Recalls something.) But Smith is being transferred.

TABLE 5.1 (Continued)

Tone	Dialogue
With relief.	CHIEF: Oh no! I'll be sorry to see him go.
Gleefully. (Now you don't have to go through the mess of firing him.)	SUP: Yes. We're going to miss that boy around here!

From the Veteran's Administration, Office of Personnel.

This kidder isn't really trying to be funny. The true goal of this message is to devalue the other but in a safe and cowardly way.

Actually, kidding is a defense. When you feel uncomfortable, you may use it to hide your uncertainty and anxiety. The trouble is that it's a barrier to open communication. Kidding doesn't really say what you mean. It's a way to avoid expressing real feelings like anger . . . and, unfortunately other people are devalued and threatened by it.

This doesn't mean you shouldn't ever joke around. Humor has an important place in building relationships. However, there's a big difference between humor and kidding. In kidding, you're trying to put the other person down. When you use real humor, you're trying to relieve mutual tension. Kidding makes other people feel worse; humor makes them feel better. So, before you crack a joke, think about what you really mean. If it's a putdown, don't do it.

If you recognize that you kid others because you feel inadequate and want to devalue someone else, use some of the techniques for coping which you learned earlier. If you kid because you feel *annoyed* at someone else, it's better to state your feelings directly, so you can discuss things openly.

There are many other exchanges that go on at two levels. For example, suppose someone says sarcastically, ''Wow, some great idea!'' this is not a harmonious message. The listener can take the words at face value, but he or she is more likely to react to the tone and attitude. And if the listener accepts both the content and the process of such a communication, the speaker will appear either confused or dishonest. That's why sarcasm, is a barrier to good communications. When you say the opposite of what you feel, your listener may not be clear about what you really mean. So if you want to get your message across, say what you mean.

Be aware of the feelings behind what you say, because they influence your body language. If you're displeased, you may frown, no matter how pleasant your verbal message is. If you're impatient, you may tap your foot; if you're disgusted, you may wrinkle your nose; and if you're angry, you may make a fist. Here is an experiment to help you get in touch with your feelings and to make sure you are expressing what you mean.

Exercise

Stand in front of a mirror and say something like: "You know, you're really a nice person!" Say it with a smile, as sincerely as you can. Next, say it again, this time snarling. Try it in other ways—laughing, bored, nervous—with as many different expressions as you can muster.

Do you see the effect this experiment has on you when your content is out of harmony with your expression? Think of the effect this has on others, when your message is inconsistent with your body language.

The "Meta-talk" Message

A subordinate asks: "Do you mind if I ask you something?" This is a barrier to good communication called *meta-talk*.[3] Does this person really care if you mind? Usually not. The true message is: "I don't care if you mind or not, I'm still going to ask you. I want to control the conversation, but it's nicer to get your permission first."

This kind of meta-talk is another two-level message—it says one thing and means another. Meta-talk differs from mixed messages, however, in that it is usually used to prepare the listener to accept or swallow what is coming. According to Nierenberg and Calero, meta-talk includes classifications like: softeners, foreboders, downers, convincers, strokers, and pleaders. Let's look at those that are barriers to communication.

Softeners. *Softeners* are used to influence others in a positive way. For example: "You're going to *like* what I'm going to tell you." "What's *your* expert opinion of the economic situation?" "I'm sure someone as experienced as you can see the value of putting our operation on computer."

These softeners are designed to get your agreement through flattery.

[3]This term is from Gerald Nierenberg and Henry Calero, *Meta-Talk* (New York: Trident Press, 1973).

The real message is probably, "I've scratched your back, now you scratch mine."

Foreboders.   Another form of meta-talk is the *foreboder*, which is a negative message. Here are some examples: "It's not really important." "Don't worry about me." "There's nothing wrong."

Of course, the situation is important in evaluating such remarks. But these negative messages often mean the opposite: it *is* important, please *do* worry, and something *is* wrong.

Downers.   Still another form of meta-talk—*downers*—is used to put others on the defensive. For example: "Don't be ridiculous!" "That's nothing—you should see the way *our* department does it." Downers are used to gain control of the conversation. They also tell *you* that the people using these phrases see only one point of view—their own. Other meta-talk examples: "In my humble opinion . . ." which really means "I'm really rather proud of my opinion, but if I said so, you'd think I was arrogant, so I'm going to get your guard down by calling it humble." Or "Believe me, *I* wouldn't kid you!" which means "Please believe what I have to say, even though it isn't *all* true. If it were true, I wouldn't have to ask you to believe."

Of course, most of us use meta-talk sometimes, and usually it is harmless. However, it can be a good clue to the quality of a relationship. A conversation full of tired phrases, clichés, or softeners can indicate that the relationship is going downhill. So when you hear meta-talk from others, try to get to their real meaning. And when you sense that you are about to use it yourself, STOP. Then decide how you really feel, and say what you honestly want to say.

The Judging Message

Here's a common barrier to communication. A subordinate says to her manager, "I feel sick and want to go home." She looks her over and says: "What do you mean, you're sick? You look OK to me."

In this short response, the boss has expressed her opinion or judgment of her subordinate. In doing so, she has devalued her and made her feel she is faking illness. And she is making communication between them difficult. So one good rule of communication is to avoid judging other people's ideas and expressions of feeling.

One of the greatest causes of communications failure is our universal habit of judging others in our responses. For example, suppose a fellow executive said to you at the end of a meeting, ''I think the boss is right to say we should cut the public relations division right away.'' Stop for a moment and think about your answer to this. In all probability, it would be some expression of your judgment. You might say, ''Yes, I agree'' or ''No, I don't agree at all.'' If you truly agree and support your associate, you value him or her and you both feel good. Most people know this and, as a result, think that the only art to communication is the art of agreement.

This is an oversimplification. You *can* differ with someone, express your own opinion, without being judgmental—and still show that you value that person. We'll be giving you a skill for this in Chapter 8.

There are more subtle ways we have of judging others which also cause communication failures. For example, many conversations turn into contests in which each speaker tries to put the other down by implying that there's something wrong with the other's ideas or suggestions.

SPEAKER 1: Shall we have lunch at the corner delicatessen?
SPEAKER 2: Oh, I never go there . . . too noisy, and all they serve is sandwiches.

The second speaker devalued the first by giving an uncalled-for judgment.

Some conversation turns into a game of ''Can you top this?'', in which each speaker tries to tell a better story. In doing this, judgments are involved that devalue others. How many times have you heard conversations like this?

SPEAKER 1: I got promoted to supervisor in just one year.
SPEAKER 2: Oh, Sally got promoted in 6 months.

The hidden judgment here is: ''You aren't worth very much, because someone else outdid you—and I one-upped you by telling you about it!'' Making negative judgments and telling a better anecdote are subtle ways of devaluing the other person. Moreover, this generally reveals a weak self-concept.

The Incomplete Message

A salesman says: ''Well I just *assumed* you wouldn't mind my using your office for a little while.''

Assumptions.   What's wrong here? The key word is *assumed*. Unlike mixed messages, judgments, or messages that mean the opposite of what they say, messages that make assumptions leave out part of the communications process.

If you *assume* someone else wouldn't mind, or *assume* they will understand, *assume* they won't feel bad, or *assume* they know something, you are really trying to take over the other half of the relationship—and this isn't possible. Even though you may *try* to get into someone else's head, you just cannot do it. Let's take a look at how assumptions create problems in communications. Jane, a supervisor, and Joe, her boss, are talking. Joe says, ''It's important to get these letters done. Put your people to work on them today.'' Jane assigns her crew the work and by five o'clock, the letters are prepared and ready for mailing. The next morning, Joe calls Jane into his office and says, ''Why weren't those letters mailed last night? I specifically told you how important it was that they go out.'' Jane answers ''No—you said it was important that the letters get *done*. I just *assumed* it would be OK to mail them today.'' Joe replies, ''Well, I *assumed* you knew they should be mailed last night!''

Joe believes his anger, indignation, and disappointment in Jane is justified. Jane may feel angry that she has been unfairly attacked—or she may feel guilty for not being able to ''read'' Joe's mind. The objective—getting the letters prepared and mailed quickly—was not accomplished. Both assumptions got in the way of effective communications.

Now, suppose the crew had prepared the letters, and Jane sent them immediately to the mailroom to be processed and mailed. The conversation the following morning might have been different. Joe might have said, ''Why were those letters mailed last night? I wanted to enclose a brochure in them.'' Jane's reply might have been, ''You said it was important that they get *done*, so I *assumed* you wanted them mailed.''

No matter who has made the assumption, and no matter what behavior followed it, they have damaged the relationship and not met the objective. So the single rule for this problem is: Assume nothing. Check out your understanding with others and you will greatly reduce mistakes.

Hidden Expectations.   There is another kind of incomplete communication which involves *hidden* expectations. For example, two of your subordinates, one older than the other, are arguing about the best way to handle a problem:

SUBORDINATE 1: We'd better get the lawyers on this right away.

SUBORDINATE 2: In a case like this, we have to work it out with the customer. Let the lawyers into it, and it's trouble.

SUBORDINATE 1: You must be joking. If this isn't handled properly, it could cost the company thousands of dollars.

SUBORDINATE 2: Nobody's talking about *not* handling the matter properly. When you have as much experience as I have, you'll understand that just because . . .

What is this argument really about? Both are operating on hidden expectations. Subordinate 2 is thinking, "If you appreciated and respected my experience, you'd do it *my* way." Subordinate 1 is thinking, "I'm afraid you don't trust me, so I've got to have my *own* way."

The solution to this kind of communication barrier is to *share* hidden expectations. Explore the feelings you have when you are arguing. When you do, you may find you and the other person have a lot in common. Both of you may be experiencing insecurity, and when you get these feelings out into the open, you may be able to find a solid basis for understanding and agreement.

The "Should" Message

Your boss says: "I'm your supervisor."

This kind of barrier to communication involves incomplete information. What information does your boss' statement convey? Very little. The subordinate knows who he or she is. But the supervisor is actually *implying* a number of *personal* expectations. For example, "I'm your supervisor . . . and I know the best way to handle this. You should listen to me, respect my judgment, and do what I say." The key word here is *should*. Many messages containing hidden expectations contain that word. People send "should" messages all the time:

- "Everybody should like me."
- "Everything should turn out the way I want it to."
- "You should do as *I* think best."
- "I should always be happy."
- "I should be perfect."

Suppose one of your salespeople says, "I don't know what's the matter with me. The VP at Ajax really went for our stuff—said he'd place a big order . . . and I haven't heard from him since."

The hidden expectation here is that everybody should like her and buy from her and, if they don't there must be something wrong with her. You can help here by pointing out that there may be other reasons why she hasn't heard, and that in any case, her self-worth is not dependent on whether someone gives her an order.

If you find you are sending "should" messages, examine your expectations. Ask yourself: Why do I feel this way? Who told me I have to feel this "should"? Does this "should" fit my present situation? Is it realistic?

Some "shoulds" are a denial of personal responsibility. For example, if your secretary says: "Please don't stare at me while I'm typing—it makes me nervous," examine the expectation behind her complaint. "You shouldn't do anything that will make me upset."

The irrational statement here is *"make me* upset." The expectation is that *your* actions automatically produce a result in her. That's not really the case. *Your* actions don't upset her; *she* upsets *herself*. She is really choosing to get upset about your staring; she *could* choose not to get upset.

Exercise

Here's an interesting experiment to do with someone else. Talk about your assumptions or expectations for a few minutes. Start each sentence with the words, "I assume that you . . . ," or "I assume you know . . ." Don't talk about anything else for five minutes. At the end of that time, discuss what you have learned about one another's assumptions and expectations. Do you agree with what your partner said about you? Does he or she agree with you?

The Irresponsible Message

Your stockbroker says: "It's smart to buy that stock at 30."

What's the matter with this communication? The answer is that using the word "it" denies any responsibility. It refers vaguely to things "out there." Here's another example: "It's too bad about the condition of our economy.'' What does the word ''it'' mean in this sentence? Nothing. This person is really saying: ''I believe that the condition of our economy is bad.'' But he is denying responsibility for his opinion.

The word ''you'' can also be used irresponsibly, when it refers to humanity in general, as in: ''You might say it was a difficult job.''

In this case, ''you'' means ''one'' or ''somebody.'' This kind of ''you'' is often a form of projection, treating your own feelings as if they were shared by everybody. The statement really means: ''*I* think it was a difficult job.''

The word ''we'' can also be a denial of responsibility. Though it sometimes brings people together, too often ''we'' statements hide differences, or try to spread the responsibility around. For example, ''We can at least agree that it won't do any harm to try'' really means ''I think it won't do any harm and I want you to agree with me.''

Politicians have become skilled at using the ''royal we'' when faced with questions by the press. They respond with ''We think'' or ''We feel'' as if they were a committee. If they prove to be wrong later on, they can then avoid the responsibility. If they prove right, they can take credit for it. Nice little trick.

The most direct and open communication begins with the word ''I.'' ''I'' statements assume responsibility for feelings and demands. Just consider the following statements by the stockbroker. Note the subtlety of the change in responsibility in each one:

- ''It's smart to buy that stock at 30.''
- ''You'd be smart to buy that stock at 30.''
- ''We should grab that stock while it's at 30.''
- ''I think you should buy that stock at 30.''

Notice how each statement is more responsible than the last. But the final statement, the ''I'' statement, is the clearest. Starting the sentence with the word ''I'' clarifies hidden assumptions: the person saying it takes responsibility.

Put the word ''I'' into your sentences whenever possible. Don't hide behind the impersonal words, ''it,'' ''you,'' or ''we'' when you're stating a feeling or opinion. Other people will feel less threatened, and communication will be clearer when you do this. Also, take notice when other people use impersonal words and decide what they really mean. If others use such words to manipulate you, point out what they're doing. For example, if your lawyer says, "It's my duty as your lawyer to advise you that we may not win this case," confront him with, "You mean *you* don't feel we have much of a chance."

The "But" Message

Now, let's take a quick look at a little word that causes a lot of unnecessary pain in communications. It's the word "but." "But" is very often a putdown word when you are asked for, or need to give, a judgment or an opinion of someone else.

Let's say you have a secretary who does wonderful work. Unfortunately, she's frequently late, so you have to deal with it. Instead of saying something like, "I'm very pleased with your work, *but* I want you to get in on time" substitute the word "and": "I'm very pleased with your work *and* I want you to get in on time."

It's a small difference that takes a lot of the sting out of a criticism, judgment, or opinion. Here are some more examples:

- "That's a great looking outfit—*but* the shoes are terrible."
- "Your writing is good, *but* your layout needs more work."

These sentences start out with a compliment, then use the word "but" to introduce a putdown. The word "but" has the effect of denying the first part of the sentence. If the parts are equally strong, they cancel each other out—and the sentence doesn't really say anything. If you use the word "and" instead, you won't dilute your compliment. You can still give your complete opinion, and the negatives won't cancel out the positives.

SUM-UP

In this chapter, we've looked at a number of the important barriers to open, honest, effective communications. We've seen how the content and tone of communications need to be in harmony to ensure getting your message across. We've seen how kidding messages, sarcasm, put-downs and negative judgments can confuse and hurt others. And we've seen how assumptions, hidden expectations, and denying responsibility for our opinions and statements can cause problems and misunderstandings in relationships. In the next few chapters, we'll cover specific skills that will help you to communicate more effectively.

6

Trust-Building Skills: Listening, Attending, Stroking, and Reflection

LISTENING

Getting your message across clearly is only half of the job of communicating. The other half involves how you *receive* communication. The key to understanding is good listening. Yet listening is difficult. One reason for this is that people speak only 100 to 200 words a minute, but your mind is capable of thinking two to six times that fast. So you often mentally race ahead of the speaker, fantasizing about other things, or thinking about what you will say next. Then, naturally, you don't hear all the speaker is saying. There are several ways you can become a better listener.

Listen for a Purpose

One way to hear more is to *listen for a purpose*. Since your mind works much faster than anyone's mouth, put your mind to work at thinking about what you hear. Listen for a specific goal.

For example, try to figure out what the speaker really means. What is his or her tone, rate of speech, expression, gestures, and posture really saying? Is the body language consistent with the words, or is the message mixed? Try to predict what the person is going to say: is he/she leading up to a point? Listen for assumptions: what steps have they left out? See whether you can use the information: how much do you know about the topic already? Tune in on *their* goal: why are they saying what they do?

This is especially true when one of your subordinates has a problem—for two reasons. First, when a person has a problem, their work usually suffers; they lose their motivation, are distracted, gripe a lot or make mistakes. Second, when they come to you to solve their problems, your job as a leader is to help them solve their own problems and get back to productive work, not to reel off solutions or advice.

Unfortunately, most people can't share their problems openly and easily with others. We fear we may be devalued, judged negatively, or even ridiculed by others. And this is doubly true if the other person is the boss. So to help facilitate the problem-solving process—by first understanding the problem—you need to build trusting relationships. Such trusting relationships help subordinates express their problems (and often to arrive at their own solutions). However, they require some specific skills on your part which demonstrate empathy, understanding, and acceptance. There are four key skills for building trust: Listening, Attending, Stroking, and Reflection, which we'll cover in this chapter.

When you listen with a purpose in mind, your attention will be more focused. Try this experiment to be a better listener.

Exercise

The next time you are in a group, keep silent for five minutes. Select a five-minute block of time, and say absolutely nothing. This will free you from the burden of having to think of what to say next, and you'll be able to focus completely on what others are saying. See if you can lengthen the silent time with practice, and still concentrate on what people are saying.

Take Notes

Another way to listen better is to take notes in appropriate situations. If you are at a meeting, note-taking helps you concentrate. Even in a one-on-one interview, taking notes may be useful. If you think the other person may be made uncomfortable by this, you can say, "I hope you don't mind if I write something down now and then. If I don't takes notes, I may get uneasy about forgetting, and lose track of what you're saying."

ATTENDING:
THE BASIC NONVERBAL SKILL

Good listening is related to a skill called *attending*, which is the way we show others, physically and psychologically, that we are paying attention and listening to them. Attending is the basic nonverbal skill for valuing others. It is a process of showing people you are interested in them, you are listening, and what they say is important to you. This meets their self-esteem need and returns trust to you. Attending can be physical and it can be psychological.

Physical Attending

Remove Physical Barriers.   You attend others physically in a number of ways. For one thing, you remove physical barriers. A large desk between you and a subordinate usually communicates that you want to keep a "safe distance." It says, in effect, "I'm over here and I may listen to you, *but* I reserve the right to stay uninvolved and to pass judgment on what you say." When someone wants to speak to you, it helps to have flexibility in the layout of your office, to have a chair at the side of your desk, or to have two easy chairs facing each other or alongside a coffee table. This more informal arrangement says: "I want you to be at ease so we can talk. I want to make *contact* with you and your problems."

Don't Violate Personal Space.   Take care not to get *too* close physically to others—this may violate their "personal space."

Anthropologists and psychologists believe Americans feel uneasy and threatened when someone they don't know intimately stands closer than 24 inches. This does not mean that it is wrong to shake hands or give a pat on the back, but standing too close to people for too long makes them uncomfortable. In other countries, this is just the opposite. In India and South America, for example, people tend to be more comfortable closer together.

Stay on Level.   Finally, don't position yourself higher than the person with whom you are talking. This creates the same effect as having a physical barrier between you. Standing or sitting on the edge of your desk while the other person sits at chair level looks like the superior–inferior role, and is a barrier to effective communication.

If the other person is anxious, upset, or frustrated, the quiet of your office may offer a short relief from the clamor of the in-work situation.

Eliminate Distractions.   If you sincerely want to pay attention to another, see to it that all distractions are eliminated. You can see to it that phone calls are held; you can close your door and instruct your secretary that you are not to be disturbed by anyone. If an employee feels uncomfortable in your office, you might hold the meeting in a more "neutral" area.

Psychological Attending

In psychological attending, you can encourage others to relax and unwind. Incline your head and shoulders forward, face the person fully, nod your head, and occasionally smile. These behaviors all show that you are listening to what the other person is saying, and convey your interest and attention.

Make Eye Contact.   Perhaps the key way of communicating your full and undivided attention is the way you use your eyes. You communicate attention when you establish and maintain good eye contact. This means that you don't look away from people; don't stare out the window, at the ceiling or floor. Rather, focus your eyes on the person and gently shift your gaze from the face to the gestures and back to the face— especially the eyes.

Gentle eye shifts that "follow" behavior communicate a relaxed interest. Avoid quick, darting eye shifts, which might convey suspiciousness and unrest. And don't stare. This makes people very uneasy.

Body Language.   Remember that all of your behavior—tone of voice, expressions, and body language—send messages to the other person. As we've said, research shows that as much as 85 percent of communication occurs nonverbally. And as Fritz Perls once said, "most words are lies." This means that the real message we communicate is through our body language, tone of voice, and gestures—all of which tell others how we *feel*.

When other people see you as interested but relaxed, they feel valued and encouraged to express themselves freely. But if they see you as nervous, fidgety, or bored, they feel you are not interested in what they are saying—and they feel devalued.

You want your body language to show you are open and accepting. If you cross your arms or hold your fingers in steeple fashion, you may unintentionally be communicating a domineering message.

Or, if you are slouched in your chair, even though you may be very comfortable in this position, you may be communicating a message that you do not mean—i.e., that you are bored or sleepy.

Your attending can also increase or decrease trust. A salesperson who looks at the floor while she or he is making a sales pitch surely doesn't inspire confidence or trust.

So remember, your real message is communicated more by your behavior and body language than by what you say. Take care that you don't send messages you don't want to send.

Exercise

A good way to practice attending is to role-play with a friend. For three minutes, tell your friend about some problem you have. For one minute have your friend look everywhere but at you; then for one minute STARE. Finally, spend one minute of attending well. Then reverse roles. You will be amazed at the difference in how you feel on the receiving end of poor and good attending.

STROKING:
THE BASIC VERBAL SKILL

Now, let's look at the basic *verbal* skill for valuing others. The term "stroking" is Eric Berne's.[1] It means recognizing others as human beings—and letting them know that you value them. While empty flattery is almost always useless, genuine positive stroking is one of the most important techniques in showing others that you value them.

You stroke others by giving them your attention, respect, praise, warmth, and/or love. Strokes have their origin in infancy. A baby needs to

[1] Muriel James and Dorothy Jongeward, *Born to Win* (Reading, Ma.: Addison Wesley, 1975), pp. 44–67.

be touched, patted, picked up, and hugged. This stroking is an actual physical need, because without it, babies grow sick, retarded, and even die.[2] Research has shown that children in orphanages often become retarded because they have been deprived of strokes.

If children can't get positive strokes, they will try to get negative ones. Negative strokes are things like criticism, yelling, punishment. Any stroke is better than no stroke at all, so they will misbehave to get even negative attention. This gives them at least some recognition that they are alive—and it is better than being ignored.

As adults, we continue to need strokes. If we can, we'll seek positive strokes by being industrious, creative, sincere, conforming. Like children, if we don't get positive strokes, we may look for negative strokes by complaining, being late or absent, cheating, fighting.

Unconditional and Conditional Strokes

Strokes come in two varieties: conditional and unconditional.

We get unconditional strokes just for being ourselves—others appreciate us because of what we are, and may give us verbal strokes like this:

- "I enjoy talking to you."
- "Working for you is fun."
- "You really are a fine person."

We get conditional strokes for what we *do*. They depend on a certain performance. If we measure up to others' expectations, we get praised. For example,

- "You really have learned this system quickly. Keep up the good work."
- "I'm glad to see you've worked out your commuting problem. Makes me feel a lot better to have you in on time regularly."

When someone gives us conditional strokes, they are approving our behavior—and they are implying that they might also disapprove of differ-

[2]R. Spitz, *Hospitalism: Genesis of Psychiatric Condition in Early Childhood—Psychoanalytic Study of the Child*, pp. 53–74, 1945.

ent behavior at another time. In this regard, it is important for the stroker to remember *not* to stroke unless it's earned and genuine.

The first law of human behavior is that any behavior that is immediately rewarded will tend to be repeated. This means that when you stroke people, they associate the stroke with what they have just done, so they are likely to do it again. And as a manager, you want to stroke high performance.

Suppose, for example, an employee makes a valuable suggestion at a meeting you're chairing. If you stroke him with: "Hey, that's a great idea, Ed!" he is likely to try to contribute valuable ideas from now on.

Stroking for the Wrong Behavior

But here's a warning: this process works for whatever behavior you stroke, whether you want it to be repeated or not. Undesirable behaviors can be increased as well.

Here's an example. Suppose you didn't stroke your employee for his valuable suggestions at meetings. When he did speak up, you ignored him. So afterward, he may decide not to say anything at all. After a couple of meetings in which he's silent, you turn to him and say: "Well, Ed, you've been pretty quiet today. What's on your mind? You know we all like to hear from you."

You have stroked him, but for the wrong behavior. In effect, you've rewarded him by paying attention to his silence. So in the future, he'll be even *more* likely to say nothing.

Here's another caution. Some people were stroked for the wrong things as children, and continue this behavior as adults. For example, Shirley used to get in trouble with her teachers when she was in elementary school. By the time she got to junior high, she figured out how to get on their good side. All she had to do was *appear* busy, and the teacher would be pleased. She became an expert at *looking* busy without really *doing* anything. When she sharpened her pencils, shuffled papers, and skimmed books, her teachers stroked her with something like: "My, you're certainly a hard worker!"

Now Shirley is a loan officer in a bank, and she continues to look busy. She feels she works hard, and is surprised at how little she gets accomplished. As long as she continues to get stroked for looking busy, she won't get very much done.

What can you do if you have a Shirley on your staff? Use the principles of stroking and the first law of human behavior to improve their performance.

You can use unconditional strokes to show people you care about them, and conditional strokes to help them feel worthwhile.

Give unconditional strokes by telling people you like or admire them and by smiling, nodding, and listening.

Conditional strokes need to be more selective. You only want to reward behavior that you want to see repeated. When an employee makes an extra effort—is usually on time, or completes an assignment well and on time—say you appreciate the act, and it's more likely to be repeated.

Stroking the Group

Of course, some jobs are so routine that there are rarely any outstanding acts to stroke. In this case, you might give conditional strokes to the *group*. Let them know they're operating well as a team. Tell them how much they've contributed to the company's overall effort. Tell them how important their work is in accomplishing company goals. And remember to give unconditional strokes. Talk to each individual, ask about their children by name, laugh at their jokes, and you'll be showing them you care about them as human beings.

Be Sincere in Stroking

One important point in stroking is to wait for something genuinely praiseworthy before you compliment someone, or they'll think you're putting them on. Most people can sense empty flattery. And don't give unconditional strokes unless you mean them. If you dislike someone, don't say: "You know, you're really a great guy"—because that person will probably know you don't mean it. You can confine your stroking to nonverbal means—smiling, nodding, listening, and looking attentive. If you behave as if you respect people, in time you may come to really do so. And if you look for things to stroke, you may find new facets of others that you didn't appreciate before.

Remember, people look for strokes, and will feel better about you if you give them. Some people may stroke others in a mechanical—or even manipulative—way. To avoid this, remember that strokes must be sincere and reflect an honest valuing of the other person in order to succeed. We have discussed the tremendous need all of us have to be *valued*. So all the judging, criticizing, putting down, and devaluing we've done must be re-examined. To be a good manager, it is essential to know how to give others the most important gift one human can give to another—value.

Before we go on to the fourth communication skill, let's look at a few fairly common situations and some typical ways to respond to them.

Bill is a new employee. He comes into your office and asks, "How am I doing?" You respond, "Don't worry about it. I'll let you know if you're not measuring up."

What's wrong with that response? Does it reflect an attitude that Bill is valued as a person? No. The poor guy hasn't learned a thing. He was anxious to begin with, and this reply only increases his anxiety. And when there is anxiety, there is no trust.

Let's try it another way: "How am I doing?" "So far you're doing a good job, but you've still got a lot to learn."

What's wrong with that response? Did you notice the "but?" It starts out all right, and then the "but" cancels out the compliment. Many people think that this kind of reply is challenging . . . that it will encourage the other person to strive harder. It doesn't. Instead, it *dis*courages because it denies the need for self-esteem.

Now let's look at a third response: "How am I doing?" "You're concerned about your work because you're new at it. I understand. Sit down and let's talk about it."

This reply helps build trust because it lets the other person know that you are interested in him/her and that you are trying to understand. It doesn't judge, question, or evaluate. It simply reflects the content and feeling of what the other person has said so that communications will open up. In short, it shows that you value the other person as a human being.

One more example. A worker comes into your office and says, "I hate to bother you, but if we don't get another service person, I'll have to quit. I just can't stand the rushing and racing one more day!"

If you respond: "Oh, come on . . . don't take life so seriously. You're a grownup!" How is that going to make the worker feel? This is a kidding response and, as you'll recall, kidding is a sneaky, aggressive way to devalue other people. How about another response? "I hate to bother you, but if we don't get another service person, I'll just have to quit! I just can't stand the rushing and racing one more day!" "Why do you bother me with complaints? Can't you see how busy I am?"

What is wrong with this response? It's an attack through questions—and questions, especially "why" questions, represent one of the most demanding, threatening, and devaluing forms of communication.

One more try: "I hate to bother you, but if we don't get another service person, I'll have to quit! I just can't stand the rushing and racing one more day!" "You're upset and frustrated because after all your hard work, I still haven't got additional help."

What kind of a response is that? It combines the techniques of active listening and *reflection*.

REFLECTION

Now we get to the fourth communication skill—reflection. We have already said that active listening is paying careful attention to the content and feeling of what another person is saying. Content is what the words of the message *mean*. Feeling is how the person feels about what he or she is saying. (Feeling words are "angry," "sad," "happy," "pressured," "frustrated," and the like.)

Reflection is saying back, in your own words, the content and feeling of what the other has just said.

Do you remember the final response in the last example? It reflected the feeling: "you're upset and frustrated," and it restated the content: "after all your hard work, I still haven't got additional help." This response does not question, argue, challenge, approve, or disapprove the statement.

What does the reflection skill do for the people you manage?

1. It immediately shows people you are listening.
2. It lets others know you are trying to understand, and you care.

3. Showing that you are listening and trying to understand helps reduce any threat others may feel; it builds trust.
4. Since it doesn't judge, evaluate, or question, the response opens up the way to further communication.

The result of a reflective response is predictable. A reflective response makes the other person feel better immediately. It eases the other person's feelings of frustration; it recognizes the other person as a valued human being.

Here's an example. Vivian's boss storms into her office and says angrily, "You were supposed to have that report on my desk two days ago. I want some action!" Vivian could get defensive—but instead she uses reflection: "You're angry because the report is late."

The boss, still angry, may answer, "Of course I'm angry—you haven't even given me a good excuse."

Now Vivian can make another reflective response: "You're *really* annoyed—I can understand why you'd want an explanation." Calmer now, the boss may say, "Well, I didn't mean to explode—what is the story?"

From this example you can see that reflection helps cool an angry situation down. Instead of defending or attacking with some judgment, reflection gets the anger out of the way. Then communication can continue.

The skills of active listening and reflection can help bridge the communications gap in all your relationships with others. You need only to be attentive to another person's message and feelings. Your response should show the other person that you got the message, that you understand. And this, in turn, builds trust and fosters honest communications.

Dr. Carl Rogers, a well-known psychologist and teacher, pioneered the use of the active listening and reflection skills.[3] He believes that the major barrier to good communication is our natural tendency to *judge*, to *evaluate*, to *approve*, or to *disapprove* the statements of others.

Reflection leads to true communication rather than an exchange of contrary opinions, with neither party learning anything. With this skill minds meet, needs are understood, and emotions are expressed. Active listening and reflection helps overcome the tendency to judge, question, and otherwise devalue others. It makes effective communications possible.

[3]Carl Rogers, *Client Centered Therapy* (Boston, Ma.: Houghton Mifflin, 1951).

Levels of Reflection

Every communication has a primary *feeling meaning* and a primary *content meaning*. If I say (pleasantly): "Get me the book," that means one thing. If I say (angrily): "GET ME THE BOOK!", the feeling is clearly very different. Using the reflection skill, your goal is to pick up both the content and feeling in the message.

There are six levels of the reflection technique:

1. *Repeating word for word.*

Statement: "This is no good."
Reflection: "I agree. It's no good."

2. *Repeating, changing "I" to "you."*

Statement: "I'm looking for a job that's more interesting."
Reflection: "You're looking for a job that's more interesting".

3. *Repeating part of what is said, but summarizing.*

Statement: "I wish we had what they have: good personnel, great product line, and lots of cash."
Reflection: "You wish we had their assets."

4. *Summarizing what is said in your own words.*

Statement: "I got in my car this morning, got a flat tire, ran out of gas, and then somebody hit me."
Reflection: "You've had all kinds of trouble this morning."

5. *Summarizing what is said in your own words and expressing feeling.*

Statement: "I'm tense about the delay."
Reflection: "You feel uptight because you have to wait."

6. *Interpreting what is said or felt, which the speaker may not be aware of.*

Statement: "I'm tense about the delay."
Reflection: "You feel uptight because you've had to wait so long. Maybe you're pressing too hard to make up for the way business is going.

Reflecting Content

In levels 1, 2, and 3, you sound like a parrot, of course. At level 4, you show you are listening by restating the message. And in levels 5 and 6 you show real understanding.

Exercise

Let's try reflecting content for now. Table 6.1 (page 122) contains a series of statements. In doing this exercise, mentally start your content reflection with "In other words."

Reflecting Feelings

Reflecting content is not a difficult skill to learn to use effectively, and it is a skill that many people have. Unfortunately, responding to feelings is more difficult.

Responding to feelings involves a process of mirroring back to the other person the feeling behind the message, which is often expressed vaguely. Responding to feelings means supplying exact feeling-level words for the stated or strongly implied feelings of the other. This helps other people to recognize and "own up" to, or accept, their own feelings, and shows that *you* understand.

In reflecting feelings, you can start your response with "you feel" or "you are." With this type of response, you ask the other person to think about your response and either accept or reject it. Chances are that if you are accurate, the other person will agree: "I think you're right," or "That's it!" Or she/he may respond affirmatively with a nod or a facial expression, such as a small smile of relief that someone understands. When other people see that you understand how they feel, they begin to trust you. And that, in turn, helps to keep communication going.

Table 6.2 contains a list of feeling words. You don't have to use this list, but it will help if you're stuck for a word besides "frustrated."

Exercise

Now try reflecting feelings. Read the statements in Table 6.3 and write down reflective responses.

TABLE 6.1
Reflect Count

Paraphrase the meaning of the words below each sentence.

1. The women do all the work around here, but the men get the glory.

_____

2. My boss keeps looking for the smallest mistakes.

_____

3. My boss told me that if my work doesn't improve, I'll get fired.

_____

4. They're always making fun of me—someday I'll show them.

_____

5. Managing may be too much for me—by blood pressure is up, and I can't sleep at night.

_____

6. He'll probably get the promotion just because he licks the boss's boots.

_____

7. Millie messed up the estimates, but I got yelled at.

_____

8. She acts just like a man.

_____

Sample Answers:

1. The women work harder while the men get the recognition.
2. Your superior constantly tries to find fault.
3. You'll be dismissed unless your performance gets better.
4. You're going to make them sorry they teased you.
5. Your job is ruining your health.
6. Playing up to the boss is going to get him a promotion.
7. You were blamed for someone else's mistake.
8. You think her behavior is too aggressive.

Reprinted by courtesy of Learning Dynamics, Inc., from the "Professional Woman Manager" program, Session V.

TABLE 6.2
Feeling Vocabulary

POSITIVE FEELINGS			
Intense	*Strong*	*Moderate*	*Mild*
loved adored idolized	enchanted ardor infatuated tender	liked cared-for esteemed affectionate fond	friendly regarded benevolent
alive	vibrant independent capable happy great proud gratified	excited patient strong gay good inspired anticipating strong amused	wide-awake at ease relaxed comfortable content keen amazed alert sensitive
wanted lustful worthy pity respected empathy awed	worthy passionate admired sympathetic important concerned appreciated consoled	secure yearning popular peaceful appealing determined	sure attractive approved untroubled graceful
elation enthusastic zealous	delighted eager optimistic joyful courage hopeful	pleased excited interested jolly relieved glad	turned on warm amused
courageous	valient brave brilliant	venturous peaceful intelligent	daring comfortable smart
NEGATIVE FEELINGS			
Mild	*Moderate*	*Strong*	*Intense*
unpopular	suspicious envious	disgusted resentful	hate unloved

TABLE 6.2 (Continued)

Mild	Moderate	Strong	Intense
	enmity	bitter	abhor
	aversion	detested	loathed
		fed up	despised
listless	dejected	frustrated	angry
moody	unhappy	sad	hurt
lethargic	bored	depressed	miserable
gloomy	bad	sick	pain
dismal	forlorn	disconsolate	lonely
discontented	disappointed	dissatisfied	cynical
tired	wearied	fatigued	exhausted
indifferent	torn up	worn out	worthless
unsure	inadequate	useless	impotant
impatient	ineffectual	weak	futile
dependent	helpless	hopeless	
unimportant	resigned	forlorn	abandoned
	apathetic	rejected	estrangement
regretful	shamed	guilty	degraded
bashful	shy	embarrassed	humiliated
self-conscious	uncomfortable	inhibited	alienated
puzzled	baffled	bewildered	shocked
edgy	confused	frightened	panicky
upset	nervous	anxious	trapped
reluctant	tempted	dismayed	horrified
timid	tense	apprehensive	afraid
mixed up	worried	dreadful	scared
	perplexed	apprehensive	terrified
	troubled	disturbed	threatened
sullen	disdainful	antagonistic	infuriated
provoked	contemptuous	vengeful	furious
	alarmed		
	annoyed	indignant	
	provoked	mad	

TABLE 6.3
Feeling Reflection

Fill in the blank with a word describing the feeling being expressed.

1. That's the second time this week I've been asked to change hours with her. It looks like they consider her more important. Why do they always ask me to give in?

   You feel _____.

TABLE 6.3 (Continued)

2. One day the supervisor praises me to the sky, and the next he rips me apart. What gives?

You feel _____.

3. I know my work has been lousy. It's been that way with my whole life.

You feel _____.

4. Getting new responsibilities really helped me turn the corner. I feel what I'm doing now is more meaningful.

You feel _____ .

5. In this company, as soon as you're over 60, they try to make you retire. I'm afraid I'll be next.

You feel _____ .

6. Where does she get off talking behind my back? She'd better watch it.

You feel _____.

7. It doesn't matter what I do—he'll never be satisfied.

You feel _____.

8. She criticizes me in front of others, and makes me feel awful.

You feel _____.

9. Every time I type one page, he gives me two more to do.

You feel _____.

10. I know it's a tough job, but I can handle it.

You feel _____.

Sample Answers:

1. Slighted	4. Involved	7. Discouraged	10. Confident
2. Confused	5. Worried	8. Humiliated	
3. Depressed	6. Resentful	9. Overwhelmed	

Reprinted by courtesy of Learning Dynamics, Inc.

Now, let's put content and feeling together in level 5 reflection. Notice the structure: You feel _____ because _____.

Here are a few examples:

Statement: "I don't know. On the one hand, I want to OK his promotion, but on the other, I'm not sure he's ready."

Reflection: "You feel worried because you're not sure of Joe's ability."

This reflection picks up the feeling—worried—as well as the content of what the speaker is worried about. Of course, you don't always need to use the word "feel." You can substitute "seem," or just name the feeling. Here's some more examples:

Statement: "Jones turned in a first-class job. Williams is way ahead of his schedule, and no one in my department has been absent or late for a month."

Reflection: "You seem pretty proud of your staff's accomplishments."

Statement: "I'll never learn to operate that machine. I just can't do it!"

Reflection: "You're upset because you're having a tough time."

When you become proficient at this skill, you can vary the way you do it. That is, you can reflect content first—then the feeling. Like this:

Reflection: "It sounds like you're having a tough time, and you're upset."

Exercise

Now turn to Table 6.4 and reflect both the content and feeling of the statements listed there.

TABLE 6.4
Reflection: Level 5

A pool reflects what it sees: the sky, a tree, a person. Nothing is added to the reflection; nothing is removed. Read each statement below and write your reflection to each. Put the content and feeling in your own words.

TABLE 6.4 (Continued)

Compare your responses with the ones we have written.

1. "I'm trying to give you an appointment . . . really . . . but it's my workload. If only I had an assistant!"

    You feel _____ because _____.

2. "I have to get another job, Ms. Chase. This one is too dangerous."

    You feel _____ because _____.

3. "You don't mind me criticizing, do you? I have something really important to say."

    You feel _____ because _____.

4. "It's my fault . . . what I'm trying to say is . . . I shouldn't have lied to her."

    You feel _____ because _____.

5. "I can't go through another course. Isn't there a quicker way?"

    You feel _____ because _____.

6. "We did it! We broke the record!"

    You feel _____ because _____.

7. "The only reason she got the job is because she's a woman."

    You feel _____ because _____.

8. "I don't like what they say about me. I'm not a loner. I have to work nights to catch up on my work."

    You feel _____ because _____.

TABLE 6.4 (Continued)

Sample Answers:

1. sorry . . . your workload prevents you scheduling an appointment.
2. worried . . . your present job is hazardous.
3. concerned . . . you have something critical to say.
4. guilty . . . you didn't tell the truth.
5. impatient . . . the course is too long.
6. happy . . . you set a new record.
7. resentful . . . you think you were discriminated against.
8. upset . . . people call you a loner.

Reprinted by courtesy of Learning Dynamics, Inc., from the "Professional Woman Manager" program, Session V.

At level 6 in reflection, real understanding comes into play. You're trying to express what speakers feel but may be unable or unwilling to express.

A reflective response at level 6 helps others trust you and feel enough rapport with you that they'll be encouraged to go on. Here are some examples:

Statement: "I enjoy doing most things around the office. It gets boring at times, but it can also be rewarding. A lot of women complain about being just a clerk. They say you should do more to get ahead and fulfill yourself. I really don't know."

Reflection: "You're concerned by the questions other women raise. You don't know if you're really satisfied doing clerical work, and you're not sure if you want to make more of your life."

Statement: "The staff is getting along so well. I can't believe it. They work together beautifully and don't complain any more. I never thought I'd see the day!"

Reflection: "Sounds like you feel pretty good. Even though you know there will still be problems in supervising others, you're finally enjoying the positive side of it."

I don't recommend that you try level 6 reflective statements unless you know the other person fairly well. This level requires a considerable degree of empathy to interpret what the other person is thinking.

But when you are able to use interpretive reflection, it will not only increase others' trust in you; it will help them to understand things they didn't realize about themselves before.

Exercise

Here is an excellent way to practice reflection. Get two or three friends or associates together. Then make up a list of controversial topics: capital punishment, extramarital or premarital sex, interracial marriage, executive opportunities for women, male chauvinists, the women's movement, politicians, inflation—anything at all about which you have strong feelings.

Then take turns making statements about any or all subjects on the list. Ask the others in the group to reflect your content and feeling to your satisfaction. Take turns in five-minute rounds.

A Final Word about Using Reflection

There has been a great deal written in recent years about the technique of listening and the value of skillful listening, probably cannot be overestimated. However, it is one thing to know the value of listening, and quite another to listen effectively. Many people know they *should* listen . . . and, in fact, sincerely try to listen. But frequently, they get sidetracked, because, as we've said, they get too busy thinking about what *they* are going to say next.

The technique of reflection *makes listening automatic*. You have to listen to the other person's statements in order to reflect them. What *you* are going to say next is a rephrasing of the other person's words and feelings. No need to search for your next response. That person will tell you, with her/his own words and feelings, how to respond.

Of course, you are not going to be reflecting every statement other people make, but this skill will help you build trust and be able to communicate more effectively. And once you become skilled at reflection, listening will be second nature to you.

Now, when do you use reflection? You can use this skill in all your various encounters, because it works with everyone. But there are times when reflection will be especially valuable.

First, use reflection *at the opening of an encounter* . . . to build trust from the beginning. This works with people you already know, but it is especially useful with people you are meeting for the first time. For example, reflection is especially useful for salespeople.

Second, use reflection to reduce threat whenever you see that the other person is tense, anxious, defensive, aggressive, or acting in any way contrary to the direction you are seeking. For example, let's say your boss says: "I've been running this company for twenty-five years, and I know what people will and will not buy. You people aren't going to come in here and upset things." A good reflective response to this would be: "You're concerned because we don't have your know-how in making these decisions."

People may indicate that they feel threatened by arguing, making objections, or in some way attacking you. When they do, it is time to use reflection. Remember, reflection is the key technique for building trust and for reducing threat.

When else will the reflection skill help you? When you are confronted with a disagreement or potential argument, reflection is a valuable technique. Remember that the other person's point of view, although different from yours, is completely valid in his or her eyes. Reflection will help you understand and clarify these views and know how the other person feels about them.

SUM-UP

We have seen that the technique of active listening and reflection, can help you communicate effectively with other people. In this chapter, we have focused on skills to help you receive communications effectively, attending and listening, skills which demonstrate empathy and understanding. And we've covered two skills which communicate acceptance and value, stroking, and reflection. These are the basic skills in building trusting relationships with others, the all important ingredient in managing others successfully.

7
Negotiating and Persuading

As we have seen, one of the most important factors in your success as a manager is your ability to communicate with others. To help you in this vital area, we have covered some of the major barriers to good communications: mixed messages, kidding, sarcasm, assumptions, hidden expectations, denying responsibility. And we've covered some skills to enable you to learn to communicate in a way that shows you value others—listening, attending, stroking, and reflection. In this chapter, we'll examine some skills for negotiating and for persuading others effectively.

THE THREATENING QUESTION

One of the most threatening, controlling, and therefore devaluing forms of communication is the question. Imagine that someone is asking you these questions:

- How would you like to do me a big favor?
- Why do you want to manage your own department?
- Why don't you file a complaint with the Equal Employment Opportunities (EEO) officer?
- Where have you been all day?
- What do you mean, you don't like it?

Can you feel how threatening these questions are? Yet, surprisingly, few people are aware of how important it is to master the "when" and "how" of using questions. The fact is, questions can be the most demanding and manipulative form of communication there is. They can put others on the defensive, back them into a corner, and often imply negative judgment. And your purpose as a manager is the opposite—you want to put others at ease, build trust and rapport, reduce threat.

To better understand how questions can be threatening, let's look at an example. Ms. Brown goes to talk to her boss, Daly, about her future in the company. They greet each other and then Daly says, "I'm very busy. I haven't had time to think about your training program."

Ms. Brown could respond with a reflective statement: "You sound pressured because you don't have time to get everything done."

Suppose, however, instead of her rapport-building, reflective statement, Ms. Brown asked this question: "You haven't given it any thought in the entire month since we had our last discussion?"

Or worse: "Why do you have so much time for other things and no time to think about my future?"

Worse yet: "Do you honestly think I'll wait until you're good and ready without complaining to the EEO officer?"

Let's see what's wrong with these questions, and what reaction they're likely to trigger in Daly.

To begin with, all the questions immediately put Daly on the defensive. He didn't do anything about Brown's training program—why, we don't really know. But to put him on the defensive at this moment is just about the worst move Brown could make.

In the first question, Brown asked a yes/no question—about whether Daly had even thought about training. In addition to putting Daly on the defensive, this closed-end question has made a perfect opening for a one-word, negative response. All Daly has to say is "no," and Brown's communication with him may come to a halt.

In the second question, Brown asks why Daly has time for other things than thinking about her future. This is another demanding and threatening question. Daly may likely feel attacked and clam up. The chances of Brown getting Daly to move have been greatly reduced.

In the third question, Brown turns Daly off completely, asking if he honestly thinks she'll wait without complaining about him. Not only is the question closed, but it is put in such a way that Daly loses whichever way he answers. Such a question gives him every right to be insulted, uptight, and defensive . . . and Brown has created more problems for herself. In her *reflective* answer, Brown showed Daly she understood.

In a situation like this, you'll get much further if you use the communication skill of reflective statements rather than questions. Reflection is one of your most powerful tools for building trust and rapport. It isn't demanding or threatening.

But there are times when questions are necessary for improved communications. So let's take a look at the kind of questions that are nonthreatening, and find out when and how to use them properly.

Generally speaking, there are only a few types of questions that are nonthreatening, and therefore safe to use. They are:

Safe Questions

1. Questions to gain specific information about needs, interests, or feelings.
2. Questions that offer acceptable choices.
3. Questions that put *you*, not the other person, on the spot.
4. Unfinished questions . . . or a form of statement in a question format.

For Information.   Let's take them one at a time. Questions asked to gain information about how a person feels about a situation or about specific things which interest them are usually not threatening. Here are some examples:

- How do you feel about this job?
- I think this ad looks great. How do you feel about it?
- How can I help you?
- We've missed you. How are you?

These questions leave the other person room to express an opinion. They don't demand a "yes" or "no" answer. Therefore, they are not threatening. In fact, they tend to help you build rapport because they show that you have an interest in the other person's feelings, interests, or needs.

For emphasis, let's reword the same questions in a way that makes them threatening, and compare them.

How do you feel about this job?/Are you really satisfied with your progress on the job?

I think this ad looks great. How do you feel about it?/Don't you agree we should run this ad?

How can I help you?/Why do you think I can help you?

We've missed you. How are you?/Where have you been? Is anything wrong?

The second set of questions is demanding. The listener won't have enough room to express him/herself. Questions like these can be manipulative, particularly if people don't want to answer them . . . and this can make them more defensive. So remember, don't ask demanding questions—particularly those which call for a "yes" or "no" answer. Phrase your questions in a way that permits others to express their opinions.

Offer a Choice.   The next type of nonthreatening question is one that offers an acceptable choice. Here are some examples:

- "Will you drive, or take the bus, or get there another way?"
- "Do you want to stay in marketing, or are you willing to try something else?"
- "Do you like Plan A or Plan B, or doesn't it matter?"

Questions that offer a choice give others room to express an opinion. They also show that you are interested in *their* point of view instead of just your own. But remember: when you are offering a choice, be sure it is an acceptable choice between one thing and another. Don't make the mistake of offering a choice between something and nothing:

- "Do you drive, or can't you get there?"
- "Do you want training or not?"
- "Do you want this assignment, or should I give it to someone else?"

These questions get a reaction, all right, but not a very desirable one. And the person being asked questions like these will feel threatened and defensive. Basically, in addition to offering a choice between something and nothing, they don't indicate any real interest in the other person's point of view, interests, or feelings.

Put Yourself on the Spot.   Other kinds of questions that are safe to use are questions that put *you*—not the other person on the spot. For example:

- ''Am I making myself clear?''
- ''Have I got it right? You want the basic report, preferably with supporting figures, but either way by Friday?''
- ''Do I understand that you'd like to be transferred to some area that offers advancement?''

These questions indicate your interest in other people's feelings, interests, or needs, and are not threatening because they involve *your* understanding and judgment, not the other person's. This helps the other feel more in control. Even if this type of question can be answered with a ''yes'' or ''no,'' your listener is not on the spot or threatened. After all, if you've got it wrong, it's *your* fault. So use questions that take responsibility for understanding and that show *your* interest in the other person's interests or feelings.

Unfinished Question.   Another type of question you can use without increasing threat is the unfinished question. Actually, an unfinished question is a form of statement in a question format. Like this:

You want to complete Phase I and get it approved. And after that . . .

Then it's more a matter of money than . . .

If we could come up with the solution for your commuting problems, then . . .

Questions like these are technically described as ''leading'' or ''open-end'' questions. That is, they are not demanding or threatening. They seek information or clarification. They really don't call for an answer—they invite the other person to finish the question or clarify your understanding.

Questions to Avoid

Now, what kind of questions do you want to avoid using at any time with those you wish to influence? The first is ''closed-end'' questions that put the other person on the spot or demand "yes" or "no" answers. They are the type of questions Brown asked Daly earlier.

Here are some more examples:

- "Don't you want my ideas on the subject?"
- "Do you think the company should spend so much to train you?"
- "You don't really think you can just do what you want, do you?"

Statements Instead of Questions.   To be more effective, you could change these questions to statements. Instead of asking, "You don't really think you can just do what you want, do you?" say "You want to do your own thing, I can understand that. However, the requirements of your job are . . ."

Or, instead of "Do you think the company should spend so much to train you?" ask "I wonder how you would feel about a similar course that doesn't cost so much."

Or, instead of "Don't you want my ideas on the subject?" just say "I have a few ideas I'd like to present to you."

Closed-end questions can get you into trouble in other ways. They give others an easy way to stall, delay, or put off a decision indefinitely. It's mighty easy, for example, for someone to put you off if you ask, "When will you make a decision about my promotion?" But it's not so easy if you say, "I'm getting a little anxious, not knowing your decision."

Often, questions are not used for their most useful purpose: to gather information. For example, we ask, "Why don't you start on the year-end figures?" When what we mean is, "Please start on the year-end figures."

Or we ask, "Why don't we all go into the conference room?" when we mean "Let's go into the conference room."

The reason for such questions is probably related to our natural reluctance to order somebody else to do something. As a result, we have a minimum of two uses for questions: (1) to gain information, and (2) to make a nondemanding, polite request.

This can complicate things, particularly if the receiver of the "request" message chooses the one you *don't* intend. Suppose, for example, you ask a subordinate, "Why don't you come in Saturday and get out from under?" he or she can easily respond with, "Why? Well, I have to do my food shopping and little John has to go to the dentist and in the afternoon I've promised my mother . . ."

So try using polite requests in nonquestion form when your message is really a request or a suggestion. "I'd like you to come in on Saturday and get caught up."

Women in particular tend to use questions to manipulate. This probably stems from our passive conditioning, which makes it difficult to ask that people do things for us. For example, I may want my husband to stop at the supermarket and pick up some dogfood after work. Instead of directly asking him to do it, I may ask, "Where are you going to be at 5:00 P.M.?" Or, "Are you going anywhere after work?" Such questions are little traps, designed to make him get the dogfood because he has no excuse *not* to. Of course, he is wise to me, so he comes right back with "Why do you want to know?" This catches me up short and stops my game-playing!

So when you want someone to do something for you, *say* so. "Will you pick up a few cans of dogfood on your way home?" Or, "I'd like you to come in on Saturday and catch up on your work."

Mixed-Message Questions.   Sometimes the message inside a question challenges, threatens, manipulates, defends, or attacks. And often the nonverbal messages that go with the question indicate the real meaning. For example, smiling softly while saying "Is that so?" conveys something very different from raising your eyebrows and saying the same words. The content of the message does not change, but the meaning changes with the change in facial expression. This is called a *mixed-message question*.

Such a question is usually used primarily to express aggression without loss of emotional control. It seems to say: "I am angry with you, but I'm not going to lose control of the conversation by losing my temper. Instead, I will threaten you with controlling, demanding questions and put you on the defensive."

One way to avoid this kind of communication is to avoid using questions, unless you really need to request information. Keep in mind that the question is a very controlling form of conversation. It dictates the subject matter, directs the other to "answer" instead of "ask," and finally, suggests that you already know the *right* answer. All of this puts others at an obvious disadvantage.

Just think of the situations in which questioning is normally used, such as in school, or a court of law. Here, the questioner is often able to exercise considerable power and control over the answerer. Of course, there may be times when this is precisely what you want to do, because controlling the content and direction of the conversation is a means to control others. But for the most part, if you really want good communication, use questions primarily to acquire information.

Poor Communication Patterns

Here are some other useful guidelines for spotting poor communication patterns in the form of questions. Think of them in terms of two kinds of questions: honest and dishonest.

Leading Questions.   The honest question is one the respondent can answer "no" to without being put down for it. A manager who asks, "Would you like to work late and complete this report?" is asking an *honest* question if the other person can answer "no" without penalty or disapproval. That question would be *dishonest* if the manager criticizes or gets angry at a "no" answer.

Questions to Show Our Superiority.   Another way we use questions is to show our superiority. How about this one: "What do you think *you're* doing?"

This questioner isn't at all interested in what the other thinks he's doing. The purpose of the question is to put the other down. It deliberately puts the other person on the defensive by making him justify his actions. And it definitely implies criticism of his behavior. Here are a few more of these "superiority" questions. Note how difficult they are to respond to and how irritating they are:

- "Do you mind explaining why you did that?"
- "Would you like to know how I'd do it?"
- "Why are you doing it that way?"

The purpose of this sort of question is the make yourself seem great and put the other person down—which, of course, doesn't work. So to avoid raising other people's hackles with questions like these, rephrase them as statements or requests, like this:

- "I'd like to know how you arrived at your decision."
- "I have an idea that may help."
- "Here's another way you might try it."

Why Questions.   Probably the worst kind of question is the "why" question. It usually implies criticism, and reminds many adults of things that grownups said to them as kids. For example, "Why did you do that?" meaning you shouldn't have done it; "Why are you reading that stupid book?" which demands that you explain yourself. So avoid using "why" questions that threaten and devalue others, and don't use "why don't you" questions that manipulate. Instead, use "how" and "what" questions which serve to improve communications.

Exercise

Table 7.1 contains some exercises to help you practice using questions. Below are some interesting additional exercises to do with a partner.

a. For one minute, speak only in questions. Every question should be answered with another question.
b. For one minute, ask your partner only questions that begin with "why." Have your partner answer only with the word "because." Then reverse roles.
c. For one minute, ask questions that begin with the words "how" or "what" (not "how come" questions or "what for" questions). Then reverse roles.
d. Discuss the experience to explore your feelings about the different kinds of questions.

Try identifying these and other kinds of questions as you talk and listen. Experiment by consciously using questions openly, directly, and honestly in your conversation. Notice the differences in the responses you get when you consciously use or avoid using questions and begin to control your communicating. You may feel uncomfortable at first, but your conscious sincerity will be an improvement over your former unconscious attempts to control, or manipulate—and you'll soon be appreciated for it.

TABLE 7.1
Question Exercises

Part I

Answer each of the following questions, indicating which type they are:

A. Do you like swimming in fresh water or salt water?

B. How do you feel about all holidays falling on a Monday?

C. Let's see if I read you right. You want more overtime but don't like weekend work?

D. You don't mind starch in your shirts, but—ah?

E. May I use the car tonight?

F. Why don't you try being the breadwinner?

G. Would you like to do the food shopping today instead of playing golf?

Answers

A. Offer of a choice.
B. To gain specific information.
C. Puts you on the spot, not the other person (or) involves your understanding of the other's point of view.

TABLE 7.1 (Continued)

D.   Unfinished.
E.   Closed-end.
F.   Demanding, threatening. Closed-end.
G.   Poor example of a choice. Other person likely to view as a choice between something and nothing. Threatening.

Part II

Are the following questions dishonest, critical, closed, or all right?

A.   Why did you misfile that letter?
B.   Will you stop ducking out of work early?
C.   What do you think the low bid will be?
D.   Do you like the new chairman of the board?
E.   Would you like to help me finish?

Answers

A.   Critical.
B.   Dishonest.
C.   All right.
D.   Closed-end.
E.   Dishonest.

Part III

Reword these questions so they are nonthreatening.

A.   Are you really satisifed with the way you've done that contract?
B.   Do you know anything about computer programming?
C.   Are you really serious about getting a job?
D.   Will you be here by 2 P.M. sharp?
E.   I can't stand these new regulations, can you?
F.   Are you mad at Joe for what he did to you?
G.   Where have you been for two weeks? Are you all right?
H.   Will you be ready to leave at 9 A.M. or will I have to go without you?
I.   Why are you always busy when I call?
J.   Do you want to hear my idea?

Answers

A.   How do you feel about your contract?
B.   Computer programming is interesting work—how do you feel about it?
C.   What do you think you'd like to do?
D.   What time can I expect you?

TABLE 7.1 (Continued)

E. What's your reaction to the new regulations?
F. How do you feel about what Joe did?
G. Haven't seen you for some time. How are you?
H. I'm leaving at 9 A.M. I hope you can be here to go with me.
I. You're a busy person . . .
J. I have an idea that may interest you . .

THE TENTATIVE PHRASE

Now, let's examine another skill which will help you gain credibility in your negotiations with others. It's called "the use of the tentative."

In trying to get our views across, we often exaggerate or overemphasize. Unfortunately, this generally has a negative effect on others. This is why using *tentative phrases* is so important. Tentative phrases cover a wide range of situations but basically they convey a more believable and softer approach to others.

The Rules

There are five rules directly involved with this skill.

1. *Never knowingly make an untrue statement.* Be honest. This may seem like a painfully obvious point, but its extremely important in learning to negotiate and persuade—especially in your dealings as a manager. Faking—pretending that you know something—or telling lies will usually trap *you*, not the other person. Eventually, chances are you will be the loser. If you are not sure about the facts under discussion, it is best to say so, honestly and forthrightly. People generally will respect you for this honesty, and this may well prove to be very valuable to you later on.

2. *Don't make assumptions or unqualified statements.* Stay only with facts you can support and prove. For example, instead of saying something like, "I'm sure you're going to love this work. It's the best job here," say instead, "*I hope* you'll like this work. *Many people think* it's the best job here."

Probably one of the most common errors made by managers is the use of phrases like, "I'm sure you'll agree," "I'm sure you'll like," "I'm sure you won't mind," and so on. When you have been on the receiving end of such phrases, have you ever felt like saying, "How *can* you be so sure?" The same ideas can be expressed without the assumption that is given in the words "I'm sure." A tentative "I think" or "I hope" makes others comfortable, doesn't threaten, and helps develop your credibility and integrity.

3. *Don't state your opinion as if it were fact.* Instead, use qualifying phrases such as "I believe" or "in my opinion," and avoid words like "ought," "must," and "should."

The difference between hard, dogmatic statements and the tentative approach may seem subtle, but it is quite significant in the reactions it triggers in others. You can add this tentative to your statements just by including qualifying phrases, and dropping phrases like "you will," "I'm sure you'll agree," "you'll never," and so on. Just by qualifying your statements you add credibility to them, to yourself, and to your ideas.

For example, don't say, "This department is the best in the whole company. You must ask for a transfer." If you think so, it's OK, but state it as your *opinion*, not your judgment "*I think* this department is the best in the whole company. *I suggest* you ask personnel about transferring."

4. *Don't try to manipulate others or back them into a corner.* Reflect their point of view and agree with them where possible, using tentative statements. Here's an example of manipulation. A manager wants an employee to begin a data-processing training program, and the employee isn't sure it's what he wants. He says, "I don't know about this, Mrs. Allen. I'm not sure I want to go into data processing." She tries to control by saying, "Listen, you'd better jump at the opportunity! If you don't get some training, you'll end up unemployable. You wouldn't want that, would you?"

People feel pressured or manipulated by tactics like this. Mrs. Allen might have achieved her objective by reflecting the uneasiness and then letting the employee decide: "You're uneasy because *you might* not like data processing. *I think* you'll gain a lot from it, and *you may find* you like it." In this statement, using tentative phrases ("you might" "I think" "you may find") and reflective statements, the pressure and the manipulative feelings are gone.

5. *Make a practice of understating.* Don't overstate or exaggerate. Try to avoid all-inclusive terms such as "always," "never," "positively," "absolutely," and the like.

Here's an example of exaggeration: "Mr. Wellington, you *absolutely* must see the new system! It's the best money-saver I've ever seen. We'll *never* get a better deal. We can't afford not to take it!"

This statement is dogmatic and overstated. It uses unqualified assumptions. And it is manipulative. How might you get the same feelings across without breaking any of our rules, and using tentative phrases?

Try this: "Mr. Wellington, I've been studying this new system for some time now. I believe it looks like it's a superior opportunity. You've said you want to cut costs, and *I think this might* work out well for us. *I'd like to* tell you about it in detail."

Quite a difference! It's enthusiastic . . . but without exaggeration or manipulation and, since it's believable, it is far more likely to get positive results.

Exericse

In Table 7.2 are some statements to help you practice this skill. Reword them so they use the rules of the tentative phrase.

TABLE 7.2
Tentative Phrases

Reword the following statements so they are tentative.

1. You're bound to like managing. Everyore does!

_____

_____

2. Dr. Blotz is the only one who understands this procedure. She'll clear up your problem.

_____

_____

3. Tom is absolutely the best worker at the facility.

_____

_____

TABLE 7.2 (Continued)

4. Nobody can stay in top condition without exercising every day.

_____

_____

5. You're going to like your new boss. Everybody thinks he's great.

_____

_____

6. The new system is for the birds.

_____

_____

7. Everyone should rise early and spend the first hour each day reading up on current events.

_____

_____

8. You ought to save your money instead of going to football games.

_____

_____

9. You can do it if you'll only try.

_____

_____

10. You're crazy! Everyone knows that women are as capable as men!

_____

_____

TABLE 7.2 (Continued)

Sample Answers

1. A lot of people I know like managing. Maybe you'll like it it too, once you've given it a try.
2. I've heard Dr. Blotz knows a lot about this procedure. Perhaps she can help us.
3. Tom seems to be a conscientious and hard-working guy. I think he's one of the best at the facility.
4. In my opinion, daily exercise is the key to staying in good condition.
5. Everyone I've talked to likes your boss, and my guess is you will, too.
6. I think the new system is for the birds.
7. I find that rising early gives me an extra hour each day to read the news. It's been helpful to me and might be for you, too.
8. I think saving money is more important than going to football games.
9. With enough effort, I think you probably can do it.
10. In my experience I've found women to be as capable as men.

Reprinted by courtesy of Learning Dynamics, Inc.

CONTRACTING

Contracting is another communication technique that can be effectively used in negotiating and persuading. We think of a contract as an agreement, usually in writing, which clearly states the expectations each party has of the other. Using the same principle in negotiating can help you avoid a good deal of misunderstanding and disappointment.

Whenever you ask somebody to do something for you, or whenever you agree to carry out some task for another person, you can follow these four steps:

1. Define the expected actions. (What is the task?)
2. Clarify the *when, how, where, how much, how long,* etc.
3. Negotiate any differences.
4. Check the match or agreement between you and the other person by restating the terms and asking the other person if he or she agrees.

For example, instead of saying, "Will you type this presentation by 4:00 P.M.?" say "I'd like you to type this presentation by 4:00 P.M. My guess is that it will take about two hours. You can start right now or by 2:00, whichever you prefer—just as long as I have it here by 4:00." This contract defines the task, and states the what, how long, where, and when (which is flexible).

The response might be, "I've just started this two-page letter, so I'll finish it and then get to work on your presentation. You should have it on your desk by lunchtime." You are then free to close the contract with something like: "OK then. You'll start on it about 9:30 and I'll have it by noon. Thanks."

Contracting is also useful in finding out if two parties are really in agreement over a solution to a problem that concerns both. Frequently we say "yes" to other people's demands when all we really want to do is acknowledge their request for our help or assistance. Contracting can make it possible to check this out. When you aren't really in agreement about what can be expected of you (or what you can expect from someone else), you can clarify your understanding by saying what you understand is expected. Then ask if that is the other person's understanding. And be as specific as possible. Don't assume that others "know" what you want done . . . or that you know what they want.

Contracting can improve any communication. It means not having to say "I'm sorry . . . I let you down" or, "Why isn't the proposal ready? You know I have to leave in 5 minutes." Contracting prevents guilt feelings that are unnecessary—and damaging to any relationship.

Here is another example of a contract. Helen's boss says: "I'd like you to work on those sales reports today. I have a meeting at 1:30, and I'd like to have that information available."

Helen replies, "The secretary is typing the final drafts now. I don't know if they'll be entirely complete by 1:30, but I can give you these charts—they summarize the data you need." The boss responds, "The charts will be sufficient for now, but let me know when the final draft will be ready. I'd like to take them along if the secretary can finish them on time."

Of course, human contracts are always negotiable. Times change, people change, events overtake us, and we bend our notions and ideas in order to live in a constantly changing world. Old contracts have to be renegotiated from time to time—not to avoid mutual obligations, but to accommodate growth and recognize new human obligations.

Here are some examples of renegotiating contracts to improve communications and understanding over a specific period.

You are a retailer normally employing four or five sales clerks. Before the Christmas holidays, you bring your small workforce together to contract for the extra hours of work you need them to do over this demanding period. You say, "You all know what Christmas sales mean to the store—the difference between a good year and an ordinary one. If you are willing to work three hours a day overtime, we won't have to hire temporary people."

Somewhere in your contract should be an understanding about a reward: "Of course, there'll be a bonus, and an extra holiday before New Year's."

Also, be sure to mention your own commitment: "I'll be working right along with you." In this way, the issue is managed. People are not uneasy if they know what is expected of them.

In a period of crisis, too, contracting can ease you through a difficulty. A worried owner of a small business confronts her assistant: "Look, while I'm waiting to see if the bank approves the loan we need, I'm pretty uptight. I think I'd be better off going out and making calls. I'll need you to take over on the inside for me. How about it?"

This is good contracting. The benefits are many. First, the owner is admitting her feelings of apprehension. By communicating these feelings to her assistant, she's free of the repressed emotion and able to accept the support others can give. Second, the owner is dealing with reality by changing her behavior. Her activities will help her cope with the anxiety she feels.

Third, she verbally recognizes that others will be affected. With contracting, the normal expectations of others will not be upset. The owner is giving her assistant a way to cope by suggesting specific behavior on her own part and on the assistant's. Everyone feels better. Roles are clear.

Fourth, she's avoiding the possible guilt she might incur if she contracted for what she *cannot* do, which is her own regular duties inside the office. By getting her assistant's agreement, she puts the matter aside with a clear conscience.

Exercise

In Table 7.3 you'll find a series of statements to revise into specific contracts. Like other behavioral skills that lead to better communication, contracting is easy to understand and easy to accept, but it takes practice and even courage to make it part of your life.

TABLE 7.3
Contracting

Revise the following statements into specific requests and add when, how, where, etc., details to the contract.

1. Can you get me that data?
2. Why don't you give me a hand with this paperwork?
3. We ought to make some plans for next year.
4. Can you come in some time next week?
5. Can you have your report ready soon?
6. It's important for me to have your records from personnel.
7. Why don't you do something about training Connors?
8. How would you like to help type up this report?
9. Let's speak to Mr. Page about this plan.
10. Will you send that application out as soon as possible?

Sample Answers

1. I'd appreciate it if you'd get me the rejection rates. I'll need it by this weekend.
2. I need your help to clean up this paperwork today. It will take about two hours and we can work late and receive overtime pay if necessary.
3. I would like to discuss our budget with you today.
4. I have Tuesday at 10:00 and Thursday at 4:00 open next week. Can you give me an hour during either of those times?
5. I'd like to have your satellite report completed by Friday.
6. I need your personnel records before going ahead. Please get them to me by Friday.
7. I'd like you to talk to Connors about taking Learning Dynamics' leadership program.
8. I'd like you to help type this engineering report. I think it will take about four hours, and you can work on Saturday morning or any evening— with overtime pay, of course.
9. I'd like you to speak to Mr. Page with me about this plan. I'll ask for a half-hour appointment Thursday morning, if that's convenient for you.
10. I'd like you to get that application out in today's mail.

SUM-UP

In this chapter, we have covered some skills for negotiating more successfully. We've seen how questions can be used to threaten and control, and also how to use questions effectively. We've covered how to use tentative to soften your approach to others and gain credibility, and we've seen how contracting can help clarify understanding of agreements and prevent communications failures. In the next chapter, we'll cover how to handle the most difficult communications you have as a manager—handling conflicts.

8
Conflicts

In this chapter, we're going to take a look at conflicts. As a manager, you need to be able to cope with two kinds of conflicts: those which, at times, you need to settle among workers; and interpersonal conflicts, including those with game-playing men.

CONFLICTS AMONG YOUR WORKERS

Let's begin with the conflicts that occur among your workers. In the high achieving organization, a good deal more conflict is apt to arise than in power or affiliative organizations. This occurs precisely because people are trying harder. They're coming up with new ideas; they're striving to perform well; the climate is competitive. This competition creates friction from things like irritation and suspicion over being left out of a meeting or conference . . . misunderstanding from poor communications . . . threat and worry when people outside one department suggest ideas for another . . . from defensiveness about who has the authority to decide . . . and from disagreements over how to handle a problem best.

As we stressed in Chapter 3, it is best to confront conflict than to smooth it over or avoid it. By confronting the conflict, the high achiever manager gets it into the open. In this way, ideas come out, feelings get vented, and problems get clarified and handled.

If you try to suppress conflict, you don't really eliminate it. You only drive it underground, and it will appear in some other, more destructive form. Also, if you discourage strong feelings and convictions, you will stifle creativity and vitality—just the qualities you need in an achieving organization. This is especially important at the higher levels of management. It is from here that attitudes start—and go all the way down the line.

So how *do* you deal with conflict among your workers? As we've said, first get the conflict out into the open. Then *listen*.

What is the conflict about? If you have set high standards and encouraged your people to solve problems and perform, their arguments will reflect these concerns.

If you have encouraged people to take responsibility, the sparks will fly from their rubbing against each other to get results—not from their bruising each other, or putting each other down. If you have encouraged innovation, then most of the arguments will be over ways and means of doing the job best—not over frustration resulting from needless red tape, internal politicking, or rigid regulations.

Obviously, you don't want needless strife and misunderstanding. And you do want your employees to understand good human relations. So if disputes flare up too much, what can you do? You can have your subordinates reflect each others' statements. Institute the rule that, in a departmental conflict or discussion, everybody must restate their understanding of what the previous speaker has said—to his or her satisfaction—before they can present their own view. Often, this will clear up misunderstanding, reduce threat, and get communication back on the right track.

As we have stressed throughout this book, you as a manager must look closely at the human side of your workers. If a subordinate isn't always as tactful and diplomatic as you might wish, don't let this allow you to overlook his or her plusses. Consider the whole person, and focus on performance, so you can get the weaknesses in perspective.

Of course, some people present severe problems. They may manipulate others, start trouble, devalue others, and be destructive in other ways. Such people have to be handled on an individual basis. You need to judge how much the other people involved are being hurt. You need also to assess what, if any, gains in ideas and information are coming out of conflicts—and weigh these against the cost of hurt feelings that the conflicts produce.

Remember, the nature of the high achievement climate automatically produces competition and conflict. As long as the conflict focuses on the job, and on doing what needs to be done, then the gains will outweigh the costs. Yes, put a high value on good relationships between your employees—but put a higher value still on doing what needs to be done.

INTERPERSONAL CONFLICTS

Now, suppose you find yourself in conflict with someone else—a fellow executive, a customer, a subordinate—even your boss. Again, the skill to use first is reflection. When you are in conflict with another, each of you has made an emotional investment in your position. Usually, feelings of self-worth are involved in the conflict, and to lose or give in may threaten another's self-image. This is especially true if your conflict is with a man. Some men will go to great lengths to avoid direct confrontation with women. So first try to de-fuse the emotions in the situation. The reflection technique is the best way to do this, because it shows other people that you recognize and respect their feelings—and just as important, that you are not upset—*you are in control*.

Let's look at an example. Ruth is a chemist in a drug company and works mostly with men. Her boss, who was her mentor, has retired. But he recommended her as his replacement. However, her boss's boss, Mr. Avery, is aghast at this idea. "A *woman* as a department head?" he thinks, "and a pushy broad at that? No way!"

Now it is necessary for Avery to have a face-to-face meeting with Ruth to explain why he has decided she can't have her retired boss' job.

He begins: "I want to talk to you about why you can't possibly handle the job as department head. You work hard, and, of course, we know your work is good. But I'd say a job as manager of a department is a few years off for you. It's a matter of—uh—well, seasoning, and getting to know the way the company works. I'm sorry, but that's the way it is."

Ruth reflects: "You're concerned because you honestly don't think I can handle it."

"That's it exactly. You are young and you have a good future. Perhaps in a few years."

Well, Mr. Avery feels better about this response, of course. But that will not get Ruth the job. So now she has to really be smart. Instead of getting upset, she says, "You're saying that if I'm patient I'll eventually get promoted. I can understand that. I feel that since I am qualified, I should get it now."

Disagreeing Diplomatically

Now, what has happened? Ruth has used a skill we'll call "disagreeing diplomatically"—which is a way of disagreeing with another, expressing an opinion, but *not devaluing* that person. For disagreeing diplomatically, just follow this easy rule: Reflect the other person's opinion in your own words, then say "I understand," or "I can see your point of view." And then move on to explain your *own* position.

Here's a statement of opinion—and the wrong and right way to disagree with it:

> Statement: "I think Affirmative Action is a bunch of hogwash. You women want to get the big jobs without putting in the work!"
>
> Wrong Response: "You don't know what you're talking about."

Such a response immediately puts the other person on the defensive—and no communication occurs. Now consider this response:

> Good Response: "You feel women are looking for a free ride. I understand how you might feel that way. I think most women are willing to work hard if they get the opportunities men have."

You can see the big difference in these two responses. The first is a putdown that just hits the other with another opinion. This is devaluing. It says, in effect, "Your opinion is worthless—only mine counts for anything. I don't value your opinion, so I don't value you."

The second example also expresses disagreement, but doesn't attack the other person. It takes the other person's opinion into account by restating it. Then a neutral statement is made: "I can appreciate that." Finally, a different opinion is diplomatically expressed.

Using diplomatic disagreement, you accept and value the other person, even though you disagree. This works because you effect a psychological split between the person and his or her opinion. You show that you value him/her as a human being even though you don't agree with the opinion. This tactic effectively switches communication from a contest of *who* is right to *what* is right. Communication becomes a comfortable exchange of ideas rather than a contest for superiority which one person wins and the other loses.

Exercise

Table 8.1 provides some statements allowing you to practice the technique of disagreeing diplomatically. Apply the rule of first reflecting the other person's opinion, feelings, or position in your own words. Then, say you understand or appreciate the position. Finally, state your own point of view.

TABLE 8.1
Disagreeing Diplomatically

If you take issue with the following statements, how would you disagree diplomatically with the person who made them?

1. I think we ought to fire Campbell. _____

_____

2. We'll place no more orders with Merrill Associates! I'm sick and tired of their delays. _____

_____

3. Sue is obviously the best qualified candidate. I want to hire her immediately. _____

_____

4. Our radio ad campaign was a complete disaster. _____

_____

5. I think we'll get there faster if we take the train. _____

_____

_____

6. It's too much work for a small department. The staff there will never be able to handle the order. _____

_____

TABLE 8.1 (Continued)

7. It's too much work for me. I can't handle it.   ———————————————

8. You supervisors are all the same—all talk and no action.   ————————

Answers

1. You feel we should let him go. I understand that. I'd like to give him a little more time.
2. You're fed up with the delays at Merrill. I can understand how you would be. I think we ought to stay with them because . . .
3. Sue is well qualified. I agree with you there. I believe there's a better qualified person . . .
4. You think our campaign bombed out. I can appreciate that. Let's take another look at it, because . . .
5. You feel the train is the best way to go. I can understand that. I believe we'd do better to go by . . .
6. You believe it's too much for them to do. I can see that. I think they can handle it because . . .
7. You're worried about not being able to do it. I can understand. I think with some training you'll do fine.
8. You think supervisors don't help you enough. I can appreciate that. I think we help many people.

Reprinted by courtesy of Learning Dynamics, Inc.

Constructive Confrontation

Now, let's look at a skill for handling people who behave in irritating, frustrating ways. This is a technique called *constructive confrontation*. This skill comes in three varieties: gentle, firm, and very firm.

Gentle Confrontation.   You use gentle confrontation with people who delay and stall. Some people can't make up their minds. They keep postponing decisions until your patience is exhausted. Other people have hidden reasons for putting you off. They stall and stall and frustrate you . . . like the people who can't make up their minds about what they want to do, or the person who says, "I'll do it tomorrow" and never gets around to it.

Here's how to deal with them. Give them some realistic limit to their delaying behavior. Gently but clearly, tell them of the restraints under which you and they must operate. The restraint could be something like time, cost, or importance. These bring the real world to bear on the delaying person. Confront them with these limits: what it will cost them if they continue to delay, or how much time they have in which to act, or how important the decision is.

For example, Eve has presented a report to her fussy boss for the third time. He says, "It looks pretty good, but there's something about it that still isn't quite right. How about trying the layout a little differently?"

She responds: "You'd like to make it perfect. I understand. I would, too. I'm sorry we don't have time to rework it because the president wants it today."

In this confrontation, Eve first stated the position of her boss and said she understood. Then she presented him with reality: the report is due today. This was gentle confrontation.

Here's another example. Edith heads the art department at an advertising agency. She calls in Jim, her assistant, who does the purchasing, and complains, "I've been going over the bills for last month and they're outrageous. How can we spend so much on ink? They must drink the stuff!"

Jim uses gentle confrontation: "You want to spend less. I understand. You know we added two new artists to the staff last month, and the price of supplies is going up all the time."

Notice how Jim's response cites reality factors—staff numbers and costs—to gently inform Edith of the facts without criticizing her.

Another time to use the gentle confrontation technique is when people are inconsistent. They may say one thing and contradict it with their behavior. Or they may claim to believe in something, but act differently.

Let's go back to Ruth, the chemist, and her boss, Mr. Avery, to see how she's doing on getting her promotion. Remember, she disagreed with him by saying, "You're saying that if I'm patient, I'll eventually get promoted. I can understand that. I feel that since I'm qualified, I should get it now."

Since Ruth doesn't agree with him, Mr. Avery is on the spot. He had prepared his little story, which he thought she'd be obliged to accept. Since many men hate confrontations with women, he *can't* bring himself to say, "I recognize that you're qualified but I'm not about to give the job to a broad, so forget it.'' So instead, he says sarcastically, ''I'm really sorry that you can't see it realistically.''

Now Ruth confronts him: ''I hear you saying you're sorry . . . yet I sense that your personal feelings are different.''

What does this confrontation do? It presents Avery with reality. Now he has to decide whether he will cope with it or not.

We'll come back to Ruth shortly. First, let's look at a slightly stronger kind of gentle confrontation to use when people are inconsistent; i.e., they express different feelings on a subject without seeming to be aware of it. Or they say one thing but their body language sends a different message.

For example, suppose a subordinate claims that his supervisor has no time to train him and he is not learning what he should. Then he says he doesn't want to ask his supervisor for help. Your response to this might be, ''I hear you saying you are not learning what you want from your supervisor. Yet you don't want to make any attempt to talk to him about it. I sense a contradiction.''

Sometimes the contradiction you observe is not in words, but in physical actions and posture. People may say one thing, and contradict it with body language or tone of voice. When this happens, you can confront it firmly—for example, ''You say you don't care about being promoted. Yet from the way you say it, I think you feel differently.''

Here are the rules for using gentle confrontation. First, *be tentative*. Don't come on too strong. Begin with something like, ''I think,'' ''seems to me,'' or ''sounds as if . . .'' Putting the burden on yourself is less threatening than judging the other with ''You are'' statements. And temper your remarks with qualifications like ''may,'' ''possibly,'' or ''could.''

The second rule for confronting is to *be concrete*. This means to focus on a *specific behavior* or *statement* that you feel is contradictory, rather than making vague generalizations you can't prove.

For example, saying someone *is* unpleasant attacks a person as a human and would put him or her on the defensive; but saying, ''You *acted* unpleasantly with the customer'' is confronting behavior and isn't as threatening. Here you avoid adjectives like ''unpleasant'' in favor of less threatening adverbs like ''unpleasantly.''

And don't make judgments. Stick to observable facts. For example, it's better to say, ''You were absent on the job four times this month'' than to say, ''You're ruining your chances by being late all the time.'' Stick to quantities you can measure instead of labeling things ''bad'' or ''wrong.''

Third, in confronting others, *avoid asking questions*. Be satisfied with pointing out the other person's behavior. If they want to do something about it on their own, they will. If you ask questions, they will probably feel threatened, and may reject what you've said.

And fourth, *stick to the present*. Don't drag in last week or last month, and tell the other person right away. If you wait until later, you'll lose the impact.

Firm Confrontation.   Some problems are so serious that gentle confrontation isn't enough. When people are very unrealistic or annoying, you may need to use firm confrontation.

Firm confrontation differs from the gentle kind in two ways: First, you are not tentative. You call a spade a spade. Firm confrontation also differs from gentle in that you explain *how you feel* about the other person's behavior.

Here's Ruth again. Remember, she's confronted Mr. Avery gently with this statement: "I hear you saying you're sorry . . . yet I sense that your personal feelings are different."

Now Avery is really on the spot. He has to deal with the confrontation or go on the defensive. He goes on the defensive by getting angry and sputtering, "Let's not drag personal feelings into this. This is a business decision."

Smiling sweetly, Ruth says, "I'm really annoyed that you're giving me this runaround. I want to know the reasons I can't have the job— without any baloney." This is firm confrontation.

There's no guarantee she'll get the promotion, of course. But she has a far better chance than if she surrendered. And at least she'll get the truth, and this will guide her in deciding whether or not to stay—or to move on to a less hostile climate.

Another time to use firm confrontation is when people consistently annoy or anger you. If you haven't been able to change their behavior by other methods, you may want to let it all out. This is better for you than bottling your feelings up and seething inside. And it may be better for others, too. Perhaps they are not aware that their behavior is infuriating you or others. Knowing about it may change them. When you express anger— or disappointment, hurt, boredom—don't attack the other. Just say how you feel. Be as specific as you can about the cause of your emotions. For example, "I really am angry that you've kept me waiting," or "I find it infuriating that you keep saying you want to delegate to me, but don't do it," or "I get really furious when you try to manipulate me with flattery."

Note of caution: When you express these feelings, say them calmly. Don't shout, fume, grit your teeth, or do anything else that will make you look out of control. Stating your feelings this way usually helps the relationship. When you get things out into the open, both of you know where you stand.

Unfortunately, sometimes people will react to this technique by agreeing with you, but still not change their behavior. They just give you lip service and continue in their old ways. When this happens, don't argue about whether the behavior is justified or not. Your goal is not to learn *why*, but to change the other person's behavior. So stick to the point, which is *how you feel about the behavior,* not whether or not it was justified.

Finally, there are people who won't be responsible for their own behavior. They blame others, say somebody else "forced" them to do something, or they couldn't help it.

You can confront these people firmly with certain types of questions which put the responsibility back onto them. For example, if someone says he was "forced" to do something, don't ask "why," but ask what *he* wanted to do. Let's say you have a subordinate who is late regularly. He makes excuses like, "I couldn't help it. I had to take my kids to school, and it took 20 extra minutes."

When this happens, you may be tempted to ask, "Why don't you make other arrangements for the children?"

This question won't do much good because it will make the other person defensive. So when others act irresponsibly, try confronting them firmly by asking questions about *what else* they could have done, or what they *might do* in the future. This may not change people overnight, but it can get them thinking more responsibly.

Another way people respond to confrontation is to say, "It's not important." Or they may say, "I don't do it very often,"' or even "You shouldn't be bothered by that." In this case you can emphasize your feelings: "Maybe it doesn't seem important to you, but it bothers me a lot," or "Perhaps you think I shouldn't be upset, but that's how I feel."

Exercise

Table 8.2 contains practice statements for you to confront either gently or firmly.

TABLE 8.2
Confrontation

1. I know today is the deadline for the application, but could you give me more time?

_____

_____

2. After my training, I've got to start at $5 an hour.

_____

_____

3. I hate to say it, but I told you so.

_____

_____

4. That's right Ms. Dietrich. This book guarantees me wealth.

_____

_____

5. I don't want to leave now. I have more to tell you.

_____

_____

6. I'd like to bring my dog with me to work.

_____

_____

7. There aren't any decent jobs available for women.

_____

_____

TABLE 8.2 (Continued)

8. I'm so overweight. How can I get a promotion looking like this?

_____

_____

9. I'm going to apply for the president's job.

_____

_____

10. Who cut your hair, your tailor?

_____

_____

_____

Sample Answers
_____

1. If you don't get it in today, it won't be approved.
2. I'm sorry, but I don't think you can start that high.
3. You say you hate telling me so, but you *are* telling me.
4. I think you're being unrealistic.
5. I have another appointment now. How about tomorrow?
6. I would be happier if you didn't.
7. There are a lot of women who have been promoted in the company.
8. This company is interested in what you can do, not in how you look.
9. You need more experience or education for a job like that.
10. I don't think your idea of kidding is very funny.

Reprinted by courtesy of Learning Dynamics, Inc.

Very Firm Confrontation.   Sometimes you need a good argument to settle things. When all the techniques for dealing with interpersonal conflict fail, as they sometimes will, it may be best to thrash things out. You may feel the other person is being stubborn, and you have something to get off your chest. The other person probably feels the same way. So the best thing to do is get the conflict out into the open. There are ways you can do this and still preserve the relationship.

First, *think over your beef* before you get into an argument. Ask yourself whether it's worth the conflict. Perhaps it's not important enough. Or perhaps it's easier for you to change your behavior than to ask others to change theirs. If you decide that your gripe is legitimate, consider beforehand what you're going to say, so you won't say anything you'll regret later. Decide on what you want the other person to do or agree to, so you won't carry on the argument just for its own sake.

Second, *tell the other person what you want to discuss*, and suggest a specific time for the discussion.

Third, when you argue, *try to find a solution* both of you can live with, instead of just pushing your view through to win.

Fourth, *keep the argument in the here and now*—don't drag in ancient grievances like, "Not only are these reports sloppy, but last month's were, too!"

Fifth, *don't attack others for things they can't help*—like their relatives, or the way they look ("You men are all alike!").

Sixth, *don't try to analyze the motives* of the other person. Stick to the issue at hand and avoid personal attacks.

Finally, *don't try to overwhelm the other person*. You may damage the relationship permanently, or provoke a ferocious counterattack. Try to make arguments a joint project for discovering reality.

Example of Using
Conflict Techniques

Here's an example of using conflict techniques. Helen and Jean were partners in a small retail shop for five years. Helen wanted to take out a sizable loan for expansion, but Jean was opposed. Helen tried reflecting: "I guess you feel nervous about the loan because of the economy."

Jean agreed, and she wouldn't budge. Then Helen tried contracting: "If you'll go along with this loan, I'll agree to that new boutique line you want."

Still Jean wouldn't agree, so Helen gently confronted her: "If we stand still, our new competition will eat into our share of the market. In my opinion, now is the time to take out a loan, before interest rates go up."

Jean still wouldn't see it Helen's way. So Helen thought about whether the issue was worth the conflict. She realized that she felt strongly about it. She was becoming bored with business since it had become routine. She needed the challenge of expansion to keep interested. She arrived at a bottom-line position that they would have to make some further investment.

She wouldn't insist on the amount, but Jean would have to budge from her position. Helen asked Jean to set a time for them to discuss the matter. Here's how it went: "Jean, we've got to make a decision on this. I can't stay with you any longer if we don't expand."

"You don't have to stay any longer. You can buy me out."

"Yes, or you can buy *me* out. But I feel strongly that I don't want to stay where we are. If you have any other ideas, I'll listen."

"I'm not against expansion. It's just that your plans are too risky. I don't think this is the time to borrow so heavily."

They argued about it for a while, and stuck to the topic without any personal attacks. Finally Jean said, "OK, I guess I didn't realize before how you felt about it. I've found our partnership worthwhile, and I want to keep it. I could go along with an investment of half what you originally suggested."

Helen responded, "I don't really want to dissolve our partnership, either. I can see your objections to the large-scale expansion. I'm willing to compromise by investing half the amount I wanted originally."

They preserved the relationship only after they resorted to a frank exchange of feelings when other conflict techniques failed.

Conclusion

When you're in a conflict with another person, use attending and reflection first, to help the other vent his or her emotions. If that doesn't work, try contracting, and gentle confrontation. If none of these techniques get you anywhere, follow the rules for arguing productively.

CONFLICTS RELATED TO
BEING A WOMAN

Now let's look at some of the special conflicts you have because you are a woman—and an outsider to the male-dominated organization. Some of this type of conflict occurs because men feel threatened by you, they don't trust women in general, or they want to lock you into stereotyped social roles. And the fiercest games occur when you try to gain power in the organization—which many men consider strictly a male prerogative.

Sexual Games of Manipulation

These conflict games are sometimes very subtle indeed—and often use sexual ploys. Really skilled male players can put a woman down and flatter her at the same time. Flattery, flirtation, bullying—all can be used as techniques to control you.

For example, a man can easily play the father-figure game—and make you a substitute daughter. Then, when you disagree, he can use his "parental authority" to win. Another sexual game occurs when a man flirts with his secretary—making it difficult for her to ask for a promotion or to refuse to do an unpleasant job. Here, the man's trick is to substitute a common male-female *social* relationship (wife, daughter, lover, etc.) for a business or professional relationship, which even if done unconsciously, gives him a form of control.

Don't cooperate by playing manipulative games like these. In business, you are a person. You aren't a wife, mother, helpless creature, daughter, or a secret lover (more on this later) to the men you work with. And no one can make you play roles like these unless you let it happen. Here are some good rules for handling sexual manipulation games:

1. Don't devalue, punish, or blame yourself. When men try to make you angry, put you down, or make you feel guilty *don't play the game*.

2. Don't devalue the men who want to play these games. Remember, they were conditioned to play their roles, too. Be open, confront gently, or ignore—but *don't play the game*.

3. Set limits on what you will or will not do. These limits depend on your job and your values, so be realistic. If you don't set limits and stick to them, *you* devalue yourself.

4. Don't scowl, get angry, criticize or counterattack. These reactions are often just what some men (and women, too) seek. Just act as if you don't recognize the game, and stay on the subject or task at hand.

5. Reward nonmanipulative behavior. Smiling, paying attention, and praise are all rewarding—remember, behavior that is reinforced tends to be repeated.

6. If all these rules fail, you can choose to end the relationship. No one has the right to devalue you by playing manipulative games, and you don't have to let them. If you do, *you* are devaluing yourself and *you* are responsible.

Make no mistake. Even though they may not do it consciously, men are skilled at forcing women into social stereotypes. While I personally believe that most men don't think about the *consequences* of this game-playing, they still do it. So when a male colleague at any level goes out of his way to flatter you, call you affectionate names, praise your appearance, open doors for you, or make a thing of lighting your cigarette—be on guard. These signals *may* be ways to put you down, segregate you, and to reduce your importance in the eyes of other men. A good policy is to ask yourself if a man would behave this way with another man in the same situation. Often the answer is no.

If you believe you are being manipulated, you can confront the behavior—gently or firmly, as the situation demands. For instance, you can say politely, "I really feel more comfortable lighting my own cigarette. Thanks anyway," or, "I don't like being patted, although I know you mean to encourage me."

The putdown I've heard most frequently in my business life has been the usually well-intentioned compliment: "Joan, you think just like a man!" To which I always responded sweetly, "A dumb one or a bright one?" Although you do need to consistently confront any and all put-downs, I am not suggesting that you overreact and become strident, aggressive, or nagging. This is as self-defeating as letting others manipulate you.

Mistakes Women Make

Some women try to outdo men in what they see as masculine behavior. They swear like troopers, slam phones, pound desks. They criticize and attack any and all who don't agree with them. And they pounce on any small gesture as being sexist.

The trouble with being too aggressive is that this behavior is self-limiting. While you may be secure in a present position, you are unlikely to move up to a job that demands diplomacy, tact, and good communication. So you need to learn to walk down the middle—fine-tune your senses so you'll know when to ignore, when to laugh, when to confront.

Role-Playing

Exercise

The best way to learn to deal smoothly with manipulative games of men is to role-play. You can get a friend—a sympathetic male friend, if possible—to role-play the classic sex roles: father, secret lover, hero, male chauvinist, big shot, and husband. (The roles are described in Table 8.3.)

TABLE 8.3
Role-Playing—Sex Stereotyping Game

Directions: Practice dealing with chauvinist male associates, asking a male friend to play the following roles:

FATHER FIGURE (treats women as little girls):
Hello, dear. Can I get you some coffee? You made a slight error on these projections, but don't worry. I'll fix them. I'm sure you did your best, so don't worry about it. Is it too hot in here for you? Let me help you put your jacket on. Take a break. (Helps her up from chair.)

CHAUVINIST PIG (devalues women):
Look, sweetie, you made a slight error on the projections—you're only off by 99 percent. I guess I shouldn't have expected much from a broad. What's the matter with you—are you stupid? Just sit down and watch how a *man* does it.

BIG SHOT (filled with own importance):
(Doesn't say anything at the beginning; makes her wait uncomfortably, while he reads some papers.) Oh, hello—I'll be with you in a minute. (Reads some more, with feet up on desk.) Now, what's your name again? I wanted to talk to you about your projections. Something's wrong with them. Why did you do them that way? (As she explains, goes back to reading.) Go ahead, I'm listening . . . have you seen my glasses? Why didn't you check the projections with me? I'll be glad to help you correct them. Aren't you going to thank me? Just make an appointment anytime you want help. I ll probably have a few minutes next week.

HERO (tries to impress women):
I'm afraid there's something wrong with these projections, but I'll fix them. Aren't you lucky to have me looking out for you? I'm really terrific at doing projections. My last one was only a nickel off! I can do this one without even using a calculator, but we'll tell everyone you did it. Say, did I tell you about my last round of golf, when I had three birdies in a row?

LOVER (flatters women):
Hi, beautiful. How's my favorite girl today? Hey, what's that I smell? You must have a new perfume. Look, you're really terrific at projections. My last one was a little off, so you do it, OK? I know you'll do a fantastic job. You look *terrific!* That's a new hairdo, right? I couldn't run the department without you. I know you'll be able to fix these. You don't need help from me. If you don't stop looking so good, I'm going to run off with you!

TABLE 8.3 (Continued)

HUSBAND (seeks sympathy from women):
Oh, what a day I've had! First I overslept, then my car broke down, then the elevator got stuck, then they were out of coffee, and now my boss says these projections are wrong. Could you give me a hand with them? Just double-check all the figures. I've got a million things to do, and I know you don't have much work.

Reprinted by courtesy of Learning Dynamics, Inc., from the "Professional Woman Manager" program, Session I.

SUM-UP

In this chapter, you've learned some skills for managing different kinds of conflict . . . those which occur between subordinates and those which develop between you and others: your subordinates, peers, customers, and your boss. Also, we've covered one of the most difficult problems you face as a woman in a male-dominated organization—manipulation by men using sex stereotyped social roles. This last problem will require a lot of effort on your part to handle skillfully. However, like any new skill, with practice you can learn how to do it—and do it well.

9
Management by Objectives

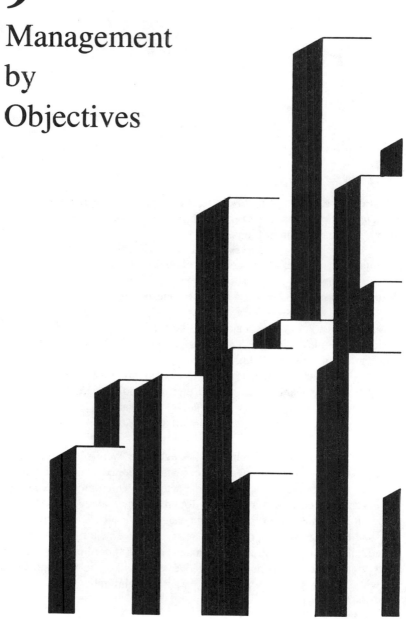

In this chapter, we're going to examine a popular management technique called *management by objectives*. Properly used, this technique has proved effective in many organizations.

Management by objectives, or MBO, was developed by management consultant Peter Drucker. In the 1940s, Drucker, then a professor at Bennington College, was invited to study management practices at General Motors. Most academic experts then used questionnaires and interviews to study management. If you've ever filled out a pencil-and-paper survey on your work, you know how inaccurate these can be. Most people tell an outsider what they think they *should* be doing on their job or what they think the outsider wants to know.

So, knowing that traditional surveys do not give a realistic picture of what managers actually spend their time doing, Drucker chose to observe what managers really were *doing*. He watched assembly lines, union negotiations, research work, and administration committees in action.

If he had asked them why they thought they were successful, most General Motors managers probably would have credited efficient assembly lines, good human relations, and other factors to which most people give lip service. In fact, however, Drucker found that the real reason GM was a successful organization was that its managers were all clear on the goals they had to achieve. So he coined the term "management by objectives." He said that in any company in which managers and subordinates agreed on goals, both the company and the employees were likely to flourish. Let's see why this observation was such a major breakthrough.

PROBLEMS WITH TRADITIONAL EVALUATION TECHNIQUES

Until the 1960s, most companies evaluated their employees by comparing them with the "ideal" employee. (Many still do this today.) They had a list of character traits considered to be important, and they measured each employee against this standard. For example, let's say a company decided that the ideal supervisor should be patient, dynamic, and well-organized. Each supervisor or potential supervisor would then be rated on how patient, dynamic, and well-organized he or she was.

What was wrong with this system? First, employees were not really being rated on their actual traits. They were being rated on *how their immediate superiors* thought *they measured up* on these traits. Supervisors were not trained to rate personality traits. Even psychologists have a hard time agreeing on the standards for such assessments. More than likely, supervisors were really rating how much they liked workers; or how well they got along; how much alike they were; or how the worker had done last week.

The second problem with trait appraisal was that even if it were accurate, there was no guarantee that supervisors were measuring the right thing. Even if the employee were loyal, cheerful, creative, etc., it does not mean he or she is a good worker. Trait appraisal only looks at what employees *should be*, not at what they *should do*. In reality, good employees are those who get the job done. Whether or not they possess particular desirable traits is secondary to their performance. A bookkeeper may be neat, orderly, and punctual, but if he/she doesn't make entries quickly and accurately, he/she won't be of much value as a bookkeeper.

MBO: MAKING IT WORK

This is why MBO, properly used, *is* so effective. It concentrates on *what people are doing on their jobs*. Numerous studies have found that companies using MBO techniques get more out of their employees.[1] The

[1]Alva Kindall and Fred Schuster, survey reported in *Human Resource Management*, 1975.

side benefits are that MBO focuses attention on results and the bottom line. It helps employees feel more committed to the organization and its goals, and lets them know where they fit into the overall picture. And it helps managers identify subordinates' strengths and weaknesses so they can work on developing employees as people.

Well, you might wonder—if it's so great, why isn't everyone using it?

Actually, most managers think they *are* using MBO techniques. A recent survey found that 83 percent of all managers claim their companies use MBO. When the researchers looked at what the companies were actually doing, it turned out that less than 10 percent of them were actually practicing MBO.[2] What does *management by objectives* really entail?

1. MBO means *setting mutual goals*. The manager and the subordinate write separate lists of objectives.
2. Next, they *negotiate differences* in their objectives and mesh these objectives with those of the organization. Then, the manager and the employee come to an *agreement on priorities*, and *set up standards for appraising performance*.
3. Finally, the manager *monitors each subordinate's progress* as he/she carries out the agreed-upon objectives, and *gives continual feedback*.

If you are not doing all of those things, you are not practicing true MBO. Let's examine each of these steps in detail.

Setting Mutual Goals

Before you can influence employee behavior or produce behavior change, you need to communicate your expectations to employees and learn their values, perceptions, and objectives for themselves. In addition, you need to identify the values, needs, and objectives of your organization. Then as the manager, you have to blend these expectations to optimize the payoff to the company and the individual employee. This is done by mutually defining and setting goals. Of course, you cannot surrender the

---

[2]H. Tosi and S.J. Carroll, "Improving Management by Objectives," *California Management Review*, 1973; Ferdinand Fournies, "Why Management Appraisal Doesn't Help Develop Managers," *AMA Management Review*, 1974.

objectives of the company to the whims of the employee. Rather, you try to mesh the employee's objectives with those of the company.

This same process applies to you in the subordinate role. You, too, have a boss. And, as a manager, you need to accomplish certain goals for your department and company. But you also want certain things for yourself—be it pleasure, job excitement, or the praise and respect of your superiors.

People, you or your subordinates, cannot begin to work effectively until they know clearly what is wanted in a particular situation. Therefore management by objectives is so useful because it is based on clear communications.

Make Goals Behavioral. The most important concept in setting objectives is to make the goals *behavioral*. To be achievable, an objective needs to be in *action* terms—that is, it needs to be something you can see, do, touch, or measure. When you (and your workers) know how high you are aiming, you will know whether you have hit the target. When goals are vague, or "fuzzies," as Robert Mager calls them in his book *Goal Analysis*,[3] they cannot be acted upon. Here are some typical fuzzies:

- "I want to have good relations with my subordinates."
- "I want to know more about data processing."
- "I want to be the best salesperson in the district."

These are poor goals, because they are vague and thus no one can say for sure whether or not they have been achieved. Let's look at those fuzzies again, and put them into action terms.

Fuzzies	Action Terms
I want to have good relations with my subordinates.	I want to reduce departmental turnover by 60 percent. *or* I want to spend 10 minutes each week with every subordinate.
I want to know more about data processing.	I want to take a twenty-hour course on data processing. *or* I want to be able to enter any order on the terminal.

[3]Robert Mager, *Goal Analysis* (Belmont, Ca.: Fearon Publishers/Lear Siegler, Inc., 1972).

Fuzzies	Action Terms
I want to be the best salesperson in the district.	I want to increase my volume by 25 percent. *or* I want to create the highest profit margin in the district.

To recognize fuzzies, watch out for abstract words like "appreciate," "be proud of," "develop awareness of," and "feel deeply." They don't describe behavior.

Exercise

Let's see how good you are at spotting fuzzies. Table 9.1 contains a number of objectives. Check the ones that are in action terms and rewrite the fuzzies into behavioral objectives.

TABLE 9.1
Action Terms vs. Fuzzies

Goals have to be stated in specific terms—something you can do, see, measure. Goals stated in fuzzy (abstract) terms aren't constructive. Below are a number of goals listed in action terms or in fuzzy terms. Check the action goals and reword the fuzzies in action terms.

For example, Congressman Wynn Bagg says, "If I am re-elected, I will assure prosperity for my district." This is fuzzy. What does he mean by assuring prosperity? To restate his goal in action terms, he'd say, "If I am re-elected, I will have a bill passed to create 5,000 new jobs in my district."

Reword the "Fuzzies" here

1. I will develop a a youthful appearance. _____

2. I will not bite my nails. _____

3. I will foster a sense of personal achievement among my staff people. _____

4. I will increase my awareness of my workers' needs. _____

5. I will read one book a week. _____

6. I will appreciate the the importance of work. _____

TABLE 9.1 (Continued)

7. I will break my nervous
   scratching habit.   _____
8. I will uphold the
   Constitution of the U.S.   _____
9. I will have a sense of humor
   around people.   _____
10. I will ask for a promotion.   _____

Answers

1. I will lose twenty pounds.
2. (in action terms)
3. I will delegate an important assignment.
4. I will have at least one personal communication with a staff member.
5. (in action terms)
6. I will ask for more responsibility.
7. (in action terms)
8. I will commit no high crimes or misdemeanors.
9. I will tell jokes to other people.
10. (in action terms)

Reprinted by courtesy of Learning Dynamics, Inc.

Putting Fuzzies into Action Terms.   Let's say you have a fuzzy, but don't know what to do with it. Your objective is to be more understanding. How do you put that fuzzy into action terms?

Begin by deciding what you *do* when you are *not* being understanding. You will probably list behaviors like not listening sympathetically, criticizing, belittling others, or attacking them in some way.

These are negative behaviors you can work on. You can measure the amount of time you listen to other people's complaints. Or you can count the number of critical remarks you make to people with whom you disagree.

Do you see the process? If your objective is vague, find specific behavior examples of what you mean. And if you are clear about a goal, write at least three examples of what it could mean. See what the examples have in common, and you'll have a more concrete objective.

Use this same process in helping your employees clarify their goals. Make certain their goals are stated in terms both you and they can see, do, touch, or measure, as well as time frames for the accomplishment of their goals. Keep in mind that MBO is a mutual process. You don't just hand down arbitrary objectives because this doesn't gain employee commitment (even though this is how most managers use MBO).

Negotiate Differences in Objectives

Once you and your workers have stated your goals, the next step is to negotiate any differences you may have in your objectives. Decide on the performance standards you will negotiate with your subordinates—i.e., how much you expect the workers to produce, how much they expect to produce. And always keep in mind that objectives have to mesh with the goals of the organization.

Challenging But Realistic Standards.   Make your standards challenging *and* realistic. An employee might be doing a satisfactory job right now, but there is usually room for improvement. Remember that most people operate at from 25 to 50 percent of their capacity. To grow, people need to be challenged to do better.

Make sure you don't set your standards too high. Unrealistic standards usually won't motivate people to do better; the tendency is to give up because the goal is impossible. So look for challenging but attainable improvements. You can judge how high to reach by looking at what your top performers already do.

For example, if a clerk is processing 100 orders a day, and your best people are doing 150, you might look for an improvement to 125 in the next six months.

How do you determine standards for departments in which it is *quality* rather than *quantity* that you want to improve (such as in service departments)? Probably in these cases your objectives will relate to accuracy, speed, or efficiency. For example, in a quality control department, a junior technician's objective might be to become proficient in a new, more complex test. Service departments usually don't show a profit themselves. So as a manager, you need to set objectives based on factors like costs, speed, and efficiency.

In setting standards that you and your workers can negotiate, consider these questions:

- What would the employee do or say if he or she were performing the goal behavior?
- What will you take as proof that the goal has been achieved?

- If you wanted your boss to judge whether or not the goal was reached, what would you tell him or her to look for?
- Do you know anyone else who has reached the goal?
- If so, what do they do?
- If not, is the goal realistic?

Given a roomful of employees, how would you decide who had achieved the goal and who hadn't?

When subordinates come to you with their objectives, compare them with your own to make sure that they are compatible—only if they are can you serve the needs of the organization. Where there is discrepancy in objectives, keep an open mind. Find out why. Listen to your workers to understand their reasons for seeing objectives as they do. They may have misunderstood the organization's goals . . . or their personal goals may actually be incompatible with those of the organization. When you understand why they have set the goals they did, you will be able to negotiate some mutual goals.

Use the techniques of contracting, disagreeing diplomatically, and gentle confrontation in discussing incompatible objectives with subordinates. Naturally, you are interested in your workers' personal and professional growth. However, you too are responsible to a boss, and you have to keep the big picture in mind. With this attitude and these techniques, you will be more likely to reach mutually acceptable goals to which employees are committed.

An Example of Negotiating Goals

Now, let's look at a case situation in which a manager is negotiating objectives with her subordinate. Jill is a bank branch manager, and Clyde is head teller. See if you can identify the skills Jill uses in negotiating objectives:

CLYDE: My top objective for the next quarter is to cut discrepancies in the cash drawers.

JILL: Cutting shortages is your number one goal.

CLYDE: Yes, I know we can do this if we make the effort. All we have to do is be careful in cashing checks and double-check our change, and we can save the bank a lot of money.

JILL: How much are shortages costing us now?

CLYDE: Over $500 a week.

JILL: So, in the course of a year that would be $25,000. Now this branch handles $10,000,000 worth of transactions a year. So you're talking about one-fourth of 1 percent. Stopping shortages is important, I agree with you there. I wouldn't make it number one priority, because I don't think it's worth double-checking everything to save that much. What else do you have on your list?

CLYDE: My next objective is to improve customer relations.

JILL: I have something like that on my list, too. How will you be able to tell if you have improved customer relations?

CLYDE: Well, for instance, the customers won't make as many complaints and they may use more of the special services we offer.

JILL: "Won't make as many complaints and use more services"—now these are factors you can measure. I think you have a workable objective there. What else?

CLYDE: I'd like to decrease turnover by 15 percent.

JILL: I certainly go along with that. What other objectives do you have?

CLYDE: I want to give tellers more responsibility.

JILL: You feel confident in your tellers' abilities. How do you feel you can increase their responsibilities?

CLYDE: I could leave the scheduling up to them, like whose window stays open, and who balances accounts and goes to lunch.

JILL: That sounds good. Now, what can I do to help you?

CLYDE: Most of my people are interested in learning more about handling problem customers. Could you set something up so they can learn more about this area?

JILL: I could give them a few half-hour talks about it, and then if they're interested in learning more, we could bring in a speaker or arrange for them to take courses.

CLYDE: Could you start at our meeting next Monday afternoon?

JILL: I'd like your people to do a little reading on their own first. How about postponing it to a week from next Monday?

CLYDE: OK. I'll tell the people who are interested to come a week from Monday at 3:30 to 4:00, and in the meantime, you'll assign some advanced reading.

How many communication skills did Jill use? When they discussed Clyde's first objective, cutting shortages, she began by *reflecting* his statement. Then she used an *open question*, then *confronted* Clyde's response with reality by citing the importance of what he was proposing compared to the size of the operation as a whole. With his improving customer relations objective, Jill used an *open question* to get him to be more concrete, then *stroked* his best answers without criticizing his fuzzy ones.

She agreed with his third objective, and on his fourth objective of increasing tellers' responsibility, she reflected and turned the responsibility back on him with an open question. When Clyde wanted help on training, Jill *contracted* with him, and from his response you could tell he was familiar with this skill too, because he restated the agreement after they negotiated it.

Monitoring Progress and Providing Feedback

Now, let's examine what you do once you and your subordinates have set joint objectives. Basically you follow the rules of good delegating, discussed earlier. You let subordinates choose the methods by which they are going to do the job. Setting job objectives is a mutual enterprise, but implementing them is the subordinates' responsibility. However, you do not abdicate your authority. When you delegate a task, you remain responsible for its successful completion, so you need to *monitor your subordinates' progress*. This requires checking with them as necessary—or whenever your workers perform something significant. For example, with a copy writer, you would review each piece of copy. With an architect or draftsperson, you would evaluate each project.

With people who do not work on a project basis, you need to check on any significant incidents, positive or negative dealings, the completion of key steps, the delivery of supplies, and the like, to see if the project is on track.

Of course, if you see somebody floundering, offer to help before they get deeper in trouble. This doesn't mean to hover over subordinates, waiting for them to make mistakes. Instead, be available when a minor suggestion can make a major difference. One of your key roles as manager is to train . . . and this is a constant, ongoing process.

Disadvantages of Performance Appraisals

This brings up the subject of performance appraisals. As already intimated, I think that ongoing appraisals are best. The advantages to this procedure is that feedback is immediate, and it allows *self*-correction.

Although performance appraisals are better than no feedback at all, they have enormous drawbacks. Here are a few:

1. Formal appraisals provoke anxiety in both the manager and the subordinate. The manager normally functions as a coach for the subordinate. When you, the manager, sit down as critic, you are in an unfamiliar role. Neither you nor your worker feels comfortable in this artificial situation, and it may damage your future relationship.

2. When you wait until the end of the quarter, or whatever period, you and your subordinates will not have all the relevant behavior fresh in mind. If you mention something unfavorable, your worker may not remember it, and be hurt or misunderstand your reason for mentioning it.

3. Finally, you don't train anyone with performance appraisals. Training demands day-in, day-out feedback if you are really going to develop skills and eliminate incompetence. Of course, some companies insist on formal appraisal interviews. If so, handle them the same way you would an objective-setting conference: keep an open mind, and use your skills of attending, reflection, disagreeing diplomatically, confrontation, and contracting. Study the objectives which you and your worker agreed on *before* the interview, and decide tentatively whether or not he or she has met these goals.

In any feedback situation, workers must be allowed to air their views on how and why objectives were or were not met. Where you agree that they were not met, encourage subordinates to tell you the reasons they feel they failed, and what they are going to do to avoid these mistakes in the future. Avoid telling them why you think they didn't meet objectives. They learn more if they have to figure out for themselves where they went wrong. If you tell them what they should have done, they may become dependent on you to solve their problems. You have enough responsibilities of your own—you don't need to share those that belong to subordinates.

One thing to watch for in formal appraisal situations is people's tendency to be too hard on themselves. Believe it or not, some subordinates will rate themselves lower than you do. If you find this to be the case, ask them questions to get them focused on their strengths and accomplishments. For people who rate themselves too high, confront gently with reality.

You can tell how good a job you've done in the appraisal interview by your subordinate's attitude. If they feel you have been too hard on them, it may mean you haven't dealt fairly with them in the interview. If your relationship declines as a result of this, you need to show them that you value them. In fact, research shows that employees' attitude toward all MBO programs is related to how supportive they feel the organizational climate is.[4]

Salary, Promotions.   One of the thorniest issues concerning MBO is whether to base salary and promotions on goal achievement. There are a number of disadvantages in using goal achievement as a determinant of salary and promotion standards:

1. Researchers have found that you can't use MBO to improve performances and adjust salaries at the same time.[5]

2. Basing rewards on output discourages workers' taking responsibility. They may stick with routine assignments that assure success, rather than trying to be creative and thus growing.

3. If promotion and layoff decisions are based on appraisals, there must be accurate, good documentation—otherwise there may be complaints of discrimination.

4. The formal appraisal is based only on specific results. It does *not* look at how results were obtained, or how they might have been attained in better ways. It measures performance on the present job—not potential for filling some other job.

Of course, you do need to evaluate your subordinates in some way and make salary and promotion recommendations. How can you base rewards on performance and maintain good, productive relations? Harry Levinson has some ideas on this subject.[6] He notes that technical skills, and even goal achievement, are necessary, but not sufficient to advance. He believes the key to getting ahead is politics; that is, how you impress other people in the organization. Therefore, Levinson suggests that managers coach their subordinates on those qualities they need to get ahead: appropriate handling of aggression, affection, dependence, and reward needs. Behavior in these areas determines a person's reputation in the company, and ultimately his or her success. This is difficult to appraise formally, since trying to do so would be like the old system in which

[4]Harry Levinson, "Appraisal of *What* Performance?" *Harvard Business Review*, July/August, 1976.

[5]Herbert S. Meyer, "The Pay for Performance Dilemma," *Organizational Dynamics*, Winter, 1975.

[6]Harry Levinson, "Appraisal of *What* Performance?" *Harvard Business Review*, July/August, 1976; *Executive Stress* (New York: Harper & Row, 1970).

people were evaluated on the list of ideal traits. Levinson suggests that there be an annual compensation evaluation based on both behavior and results. This would include a review of whether or not employees have met their goals, how they have handled their responsibilities, whether they solved problems, and whether they turned a profit.

Levinson believes that there is a difference between behavior and results. This would include a review of whether or not employees have met their goals, how they have handled their responsibilities, whether they didn't respond to changes with enough speed or flexibility. Or they may have gotten the right results on any easy job without too much effort, but could still improve their performance. In any case, separating behavior from results allows a manager to reward subordinates appropriately, while leaving the manager free to develop them.

MAKING ORGANIZATIONAL
AND INDIVIDUAL GOALS MESH

As we have seen, people are most motivated by objectives they determine for themselves. However, the needs and desires of workers have to be fit in with the overall goals of your department and the company. One of the benefits of MBO is that it shows people how they fit into the big picture, thus making it easier for them to determine realistic, effective goals. Balancing *their* objectives with those of the organization helps people feel valued. So you, as a manager, need to be particularly aware of your organization's goals, and to set your own goals accordingly.

Too often, managers look only at the goals and performance in their own little niche, and not how it relates to overall company goals. The sales manager may look only at units sold, the production manager at productivity, the R&D manager at new products, and the safety manager only at accident rates. The result can be chaos for the organization as a whole, because each manager protects his or her little empire. For effective MBO, you need to mesh goals . . . the organization's, yours, and those of your subordinates.

YOUR GOALS AND PRIORITIES

If you work for an organization that sets formal goals, your goal-setting job is easier. But what if your organization doesn't have a formal goal-setting procedure? How do you set your goals? The rule here is to "watch what they do." To learn what top management values, keep your eyes and ears open to see what performances are rewarded. For example, to what departments are the big budgets being allocated? Who is being promoted? What are the people in power doing? Use your mentor and your informal network connections to learn the current top priorities.

EFFICIENCY VS. EFFECTIVENESS

In setting your goals and priorities, keep in mind that as a manager, in addition to administering, you need to be an entrepreneur. That is, you have to redirect resources from areas of low or declining results to areas of high or increasing results. So you need to understand the difference between efficiency and effectiveness. Efficiency is similar to productivity—doing the fastest job at the lowest cost. Effectiveness, on the other hand, is doing the *right* job. Workers may be very efficient, but if what they are doing doesn't contribute to the organization's effectiveness, their efforts are wasted. Effectiveness means focusing on the most profitable products or services and the most profitable markets.

In thinking about effectiveness, keep in mind the "80/20 rule": 20 percent of any activity usually accounts for 80 percent of the results.[7] (For example, 20 percent of the workers generally cause about 80 percent of the problems; 20 percent of the customers probably account for 80 percent of your revenue, and so on.) If you can find the 20 percent of your division's activities that contribute to 80 percent of your results, you can become more effective by making these your top priorities. This is important in

[7]Peter H. Drucker, *Management Tasks, Responsibilities, Practices* (New York: Harper & Row, 1973), pp. 45–46.

establishing your goals. You might even be able to reduce the 80 percent of your time you may spend on unimportant activities, whether it's filling out forms, calling on small customers, or handling inquiries personally.

As Drucker points out, "Even the healthiest business, the business with the greatest effectiveness, can well die of poor efficiency. But even the most efficient business cannot survive, let alone succeed, if it is efficient in doing the wrong things, that is, if it lacks effectiveness. No amount of efficiency would have enabled the manufacturer of buggy whips to survive. Effectiveness is the foundation of success—efficiency is a minimum for survival *after* success has been achieved."[8]

UPWARD APPRAISAL

One of the newest practices in the field of organizational development is upward appraisal: your subordinates appraise you. This is a process of learning what help your subordinates need from you to reach their goals and what *you do* that may hinder them. And if you think this means you'll lose face or that as the manager *you* should be doing all the evaluating, take a look at reality.

Your subordinates already do evaluate you, at least among themselves. It's helpful to find out what this evaluation is. You probably have a pretty good idea about how they evaluate you now, from their performances. If their work is sloppy or careless, that tells you how they may be responding to your leadership. If they work hard, they are probably well motivated by you. Asking them what you do that helps and hinders them brings their evaluations out into the open. Then you can correct any of your actions or procedures that may be preventing them from clearly understanding your goals and company goals.

One word of caution: don't spring this request for evaluation on subordinates all of a sudden. If you ask them what they think of you out of the blue, you will catch them off guard and they may not be frank with you. Instead, you can start by asking them how they appraise managers generally, or how they see your job. Once they have defined the criteria for

[8]Ibid.

evaluating your job, and trust you, you can ask them to give you some idea of how they regard your performance specifically. Working up to this gradually is less likely to threaten them.

Through this process of upward appraisal, you may unearth some important information that will help you grow as a manager. For example, you may learn that you demand both speed and high quality, both of which may not be possible. Or you may learn that although you encourage taking individual responsibility, you really expect subordinates to check with you before they make any decisions. This automatically limits their growth—*and* yours.

Your Perception
of Boss'/Company's Goals

You may find such inconsistencies in your own perceptions of *your* boss' goals and behavior. If so, you can use gentle confrontation techniques to get a clearer understanding. Lay out the statements and actions side by side, and ask your boss to resolve them. Remember, in using gentle confrontation be tentative, mention objective behavior, and refer to reality. Setting mutual objectives with your boss helps both of you focus on the outputs the job demands, not just the behaviors that the boss favors.

Concerning this, Silber and Sherman write:[9]

> In the subordinate role, one continuing concern is trying to determine what it takes to please the old man, what it takes to relieve the anxieties that you have about his expectations of you. The answer to that comes through confrontation, sincerity, and management by objectives. . . . Employees are willing to perform if only someone would tell them what is desired and what is expected of them. . . . If an employee is motivationally geared up, if he works well with authority, if he is willing to take risks, if his past experience is positive and contributory, and if the ethical values are aligned with yours—but he doesn't understand what you want—then his performance will suffer and he will be frustrated.

[9]Mark B. Silber and V. Clayton Sherman, *Managerial Performance and Promotability: The Making of an Executive* (New York: American Management Assn., Inc., 1974), pp. 37–38.

CAUTIONS ABOUT MBO

Finally, some cautions about MBO. It can't do your job of managing for you. It can only make you more effective *if* you use it properly. Here are some things to watch out for when you are using the MBO technique:

1. Don't expect MBO to change your leadership style, nor your relationships with subordinates, their amount of participation, the nature of feedback, or workers trust in you. You can do all these things, but MBO won't do them for you.

2. Make sure the goals are clear and mutually understood.

3. Don't forget to follow up your goal-setting by checking progress.

4. Establish a trusting relationship with your workers *before* you get into MBO. Otherwise, subordinates will feel threatened and resist it.

5. Be sure you set goals that have top priorities for the company.

With these guidelines in mind, you will find management by objectives an effective and rewarding technique to use in your managing.

SUM-UP

In this chapter, we have examined the popular management technique of management by objectives or MBO. We have covered the way to use the MBO process correctly, which is a mutual process between you and your subordinates as well as between you and your boss to set and mesh individual and organizational goals. We've covered some specific skills to implement MBO and seen some of the problems and limitations of using MBO effectively.

10
Decision-Making

In an earlier chapter, we discussed the job of managing in terms of ten basic roles which are either interpersonal, information getting or decision-making. While all of the functions are necessary and no one of them can be ignored, probably the single most important one—and often the most difficult—is that of decision-maker. And to make effective decisions, you need to gain power.

THE INFORMAL SYSTEM
OF RELATIONSHIPS

The fact that most women are outsiders in the organization has a direct impact on their skill in making decisions, because in reality, the organization consists of an informal system of relationships. And through this system men have (at lunch, on the golf course, in the men's room) access to vast amounts of information which they use as inputs to decision-making.

So, before we talk about the process of decision-making, let's take a look at you, as a woman in the organization.

Who Are You in the Organization?

Who are *you* in this informal system of relationships—a system that surrounds the formal positions on an organizational chart? How are you seen? By whom? How helpful, useful, important can these people be to you, and vice versa?

As outsiders, women often fail to take this informal system seriously. And women who do recognize its importance often don't know how to deal with it. "Dealing with it" means developing relationships with people in the organization over and beyond those you see every day. Ask yourself these questions:

- What position are you aiming for next?
- Who could help you get it?
- Who has the information you need to make good decisions?
- How do they see you?
- How can you establish better relationships with them?

Women often try to succeed in the organization by creating their own little empire in which they aren't dependent on others. This is a serious mistake in strategy. Not only does it lock you into that little empire—perhaps for good—but it conflicts directly with the requirements of a manager's job. Managing is coordinating and leading and making decisions for, and with, other people. And this demands the ability to trust in, depend on, communicate with, and delegate to others—particularly your peers and subordinates. But because you are an outsider, this game is not so easy to learn to play.

How will you learn?

Unfortunately, there are no quick steps, no easy formula. It boils down to establishing relationships with your co-managers and, if possible, more senior managers, who can steer you and give you inside information and warn you of impending changes. You need to gather information from within the informal system, and this means you have to understand the climate in your organization and develop relationships within it.

Begin by assessing the kind of organizational climate that exists (formal, informal, achievement, or some combination) and learning the written and unwritten rules of the climate.

Climate of Your Organization

Some organizations are so tightly structured that their rules extend right into their employees' personal lives. There are unwritten, but nonetheless well-understood "rules" of behavior expected of employees—

especially of those employees known as "comers." Your lifestyle—the way you dress, where you live, the car you drive, who you entertain, the clubs you join—all affect your career rise in certain companies.

At the other end of the scale are the organizations in which the lifestyle of employees is immaterial. You can do your own thing as long as you produce results.

Some job climates repress employees to the point of withdrawal. Knowing there is no interpersonal trust and that conflicts will be punished, employees make no emotional commitment, render no decisions, take no risks, and make no waves. They conform to the existing structure.

Still other job climates are jungles. All behavior is based on survival of the fittest. In these places, there is a rough, no-holds-barred game. Emotions are high, the atmosphere is charged, and to the victor goes the ball game—until he or she is beaten by someone else.

Of course, these are the extremes. But these organizational climates and every variation in between do exist. Become aware of the values that are accepted or not accepted in your organization. Do these values coincide with your own? Can you live with them and still perform effectively? If not, a job change may be in order. However, if the climate is comfortable for you, stay in tune with the expected behavior, but stay flexible. Rules and climates can change with a change of leaders.

Just as organizational climate and the standards for accepted behavior can change, so can the interpersonal relationships you establish. You need to form relationships with those whose values and needs coincide with yours. These relationships play an important part in your information-gathering as well as your promotability. You are establishing political contacts and building a sponsorship that helps you get your ideas accepted and implemented. This, in turn, affects your decisions, your performance, and your continued career rise.

Be Aware of Organizational Politics

Yes, *politics*—exist at every level of management. The cliché "it's not what you know, but who you know" is as true in the organizational world as in the rest of life. You may deplore its existence, but refusing to recognize and deal with this reality can hurt you.

You can do everything according to the book, apply all the latest management-effectiveness theories, and still be ineffective. If you remain blind to, or prefer to "stay above" organizational politics, if you cannot handle the doubt or anxiety, or if you find you cannot keep your senses tuned to what's *really* happening within your environment, perhaps a career in a large-scale organization is not for you. There are those who thrive in this situation. Only you know if you are one of these people.

Realists see organizational politics as oil on the wheels of progress. They recognize who has the influence and power to make changes or get ideas acted on. They make tradeoffs, negotiate, use their own leverage, or realign their position with others in order to get results. And most of all they gain information that helps them make decisions.

Know Who Has the Power.   So stay aware of the shifting grouping and regrouping, as well as the informal "understandings" that exist between people. Know the relationships that have formed or dissolved. This is a necessary part of being a successful manager. You need to know who has the power now, and who may have it next month. Who's likely to be promoted to a particular job? Is it someone you know, and will this promotion affect your areas of responsibility in any way?

You need to know who has the contacts, who to see to get something done, and who has the real power. Is it the person with the title, or is it actually someone else? You need to know who has lost power and no longer has the influence to be effective. And don't let titles or status symbols fool you.

How can political awareness help you? Let's look at an example. Let's say you have a potential sale that can double your department's performance over last year—*if* you can get the goods to the client immediately. You could go through the system and keep your fingers crossed that the order will reach the shipping department and be handled promptly. Or you can use your awareness of who has the power to put your order ahead of everyone else's. Or, if you've laid the groundwork, you've already established an informal relationship with the head of the production and shipping department and can make your own tradeoff.

Pay Your Debts, Keep Your Word.   Your coalitions, negotiations, and tradeoffs require two vitally important things:

1. Pay off your organizational debts
2. Keep your word

When someone does you a favor, recognize that you are expected to return that favor in the future. Not doing so may ruin your credibility, damage your reputation, and undermine your career.

The same is true when you refuse to keep your word. If you make a commitment to back someone, follow through. Withdrawing your promised support in an informal arrangement leaves the other person standing alone. So you can expect to be repaid in kind in the future.

Keep Your Ears Open.   In his book,[1] Michael Korda gives women this advice:

> Women have, in any case, certain advantages over men. In the first place, men are seldom inclined to see them as rivals, male chauvinist pride being what it is. In power struggles, they consistently underrate women. Worse, men talk too much. Even those who have learned to keep their mouths shut in front of other men (and they are few) will talk openly in front of a woman, supposing that she is automatically "on their side." There is a natural tendency to *confide* in women, as if they were destined by nature to be approving listeners, and any intelligent woman can exploit this fairly easily, no more being necessary than a sympathetic air and a few words of encouragement. It is astonishing that men who won't tell their colleagues anything will tell a woman everything.

So keep your ears open. Pay attention and listen. If you do, you'll know more about what's happening than most men. And this, in turn, will greatly enrich your information inputs into your decisions.

BUILDING RELATIONSHIPS

Now let's see how you can build relationships within the informal organization.

Louis Rutherberg said, "Our greatest opportunities for advancing productivity and improving living standards are to be found in the field of human relationships."[2]

---

[1] Michael Korda, *Power! How to Get it, How to Use It* (New York: Random House, 1975), p. 239.

[2] "Forbes Scrapbook of Thoughts on Business Life," B.G. Forbes & Sons Publishing Co., Inc., Forbes, Inc., New York, 1950.

And Douglas McGregor wrote, "The outstanding characteristics of the relationship between subordinates and superiors is the subordinate's dependence upon superiors for the satisfaction of their needs."[3]

Everything in life is affected by relationships—it is the interdependence of many minds and many efforts that is responsible for American ingenuity, innovation, productivity, and performance.

You as a manager need to develop relationships with your peers and senior managers—both to gain visibility and to gather information to make decisions. You also need to develop relationships with your workers. As a manager, you depend on your subordinates to get the job done. Your subordinates, in turn, depend on you to satisfy their needs and help them grow. Techniques for improving human relationships can enrich and broaden your opportunities to solve problems, increase production and profit, and enhance the personal growth and satisfaction of yourself and your workers.

TABLE 10.1
Distancing Evaluation

Do you keep other people at arm's length? Distancing interferes with building great relationships. How much of it do you do?

	OFTEN	SOMETIMES	SELDOM	NEVER
1. I like to keep my feelings to myself.				
2. I use clothes to create different impressions.				
3. I'm afraid of what people would think if they really knew me.				
4. I'm embarrassed when I have to praise people.				
5. I don't like people to touch me.				
6. I have to know people a long time before I can trust them.				
7. I have a pet theory I like to explain.				
8. I prefer to be by myself.				

[3]Robert M. Wald and Roy A. Doty, "The Top Executive—A Firsthand Profile," "Skills That Build Executive Success"—Reprints from *Harvard Business Review*, Harvard College, 1954–1964.

TABLE 10.1 (Continued)

	OFTEN	SOMETIMES	SELDOM	NEVER
9. I answer questions with a simple "yes" or "no."	_____	_____	_____	_____
10. I wait for others to speak to me first.	_____	_____	_____	_____
11. I look for faults in others.	_____	_____	_____	_____
12. I prefer a lot of acquaintances to a few close friends.	_____	_____	_____	_____
13. I'm afraid of being hurt in a relationship.	_____	_____	_____	_____
14. I like to analyze other people.	_____	_____	_____	_____
15. I can't really relax with someone until we've had a few drinks.	_____	_____	_____	_____
16. The demands of my job or hobby leave little time for socializing.	_____	_____	_____	_____
17. I always wear the same expression on my face.	_____	_____	_____	_____
18. I enjoy kidding people.	_____	_____	_____	_____
19. I enjoy a good argument.	_____	_____	_____	_____
20. I don't let anyone get away with a mistake.	_____	_____	_____	_____

Score

Score *Often* as 5; *Sometimes* as 3; *Seldom* as 1, and *Never* as 0. Add up your score and rate yourself as follows:

0–25   You are very open.
26–50   You are fairly open, with some distancing.
51–75   You tend to build barriers with people.
76–100 You seem to do a great deal of distancing.

Barriers to Forming Good Relationships

Let's examine some of the behaviors that can create barriers to forming positive relationships. Then we'll see how you can build honest, open, trusting relationships with others.

Distancing.   One formidable barrier to creating good relationships is a behavior called *distancing*. This is a way of keeping others away from us. Most of us over the age of 30 have been taught this practice by society. For men it has been considered a sign of strength to hide feelings. And women have been taught to be passive and compliant, and to suffer in silence.

One way Americans "distance" others is to put on masks to portray different roles. We behave in one way with family, another with colleagues, and still another with friends. How we act depends in part on what we think other people *expect* from us. For example, you may clown around with your children, but you would probably be embarrassed to have your boss see this behavior. You may act tough with a subordinate because you think that's the best way to get him to cooperate, but be charming with a customer because you think that's how to get more business. In other words, we give impressions of what we *think* will impress or influence other people.

Use of Props.   Another barrier to forming good relationships concerns the use of *props*. Just as we are in a sense actors with masks and different roles to play, so we use props as a performer might. We may use clothes to create an image—like the older woman who dresses in clothes that are overly youthful. She's saying "I want you to think that I'm younger than I really am, that I'm 'with it.' " The young executive who wears conservative clothes may be saying, "I want you to think that I'm conventional, straightforward, trustworthy."

We may use props like Phi Beta Kappa keys, pants suits, frilly blouses, jewelry to tell the world something. Of course, we need to dress with care, and show ourselves to best advantage. But when we use props to create a false image, we are creating another barrier to relationships with others. And most people are not impressed by distancing props for very long.

Ego Needs.   Finally, the most destructive barrier to open, honest relationships probably concerns our own ego needs. In order to hide the fact that we are not perfect—whatever perfect is—we play games. At one extreme we may brag, pull rank, or become defensive when we suspect that others don't respect or appreciate us. At the other extreme, we may be lonely and shy, think others are being snobs, play helpless, or manipulate others. Either way, such behavior can put a lot of distance between us and other people.

Unfortunately, distancing can negatively affect our relationships.

The New Openness

In the 1960s, our children recognized the phoniness and destructiveness of our ways. They refused to accept our values. They even threatened our comfortable status quo—the things many of us considered "right" behavior. But now, gradually, our cultural value system is shifting from distance to closeness, from closed to open, from hiding or denying feelings to expressing and valuing them.

Today you're more apt to hear "Have a good day" than "So long." Many of the putdown phrases a few years back ("Drop dead!" "Get lost!") have vanished, and given way to everyday exchanges of support.

Taking Risks

Even so, many adults find it difficult or even impossible to develop open, honest relationships . . . unless they have known others for years. This is understandable, because many people have been taught to believe that to be open involves risk. Revealing your true self means telling someone else about your feelings, your experiences, your fears, ideas, fantasies, your hangups and problems, your hopes and your dreams. If you don't fully trust the other person, it might be because you fear being rejected or betrayed or taken advantage of.

But does being open, relating warmly, and caring about others really involve much risk? If you honestly feel it does, ask yourself, "What kind of risk?" If the other person doesn't listen or doesn't care, is it so bad? Actually, it doesn't hurt you—maybe it means the other person isn't worth your efforts. And it's better for you to discover this early in a relationship, rather than wasting your time and perhaps being disappointed later on.

Suppose the person you open up to *does* tell others what you've revealed. If you accept yourself, you have nothing to fear from other people knowing what and who you really are. In fact, we now know that the better other people know us, generally, the more they like and trust us and the less they fear us. Remember, building trusting relationships is the single most important factor in successfully managing and motivating others.

For example, in a recent *Harvard Business Review* study, people at the top of America's leading corporations named the ability to relate well and communicate with others as the single most important factor in their success.[4]

Exercise

How much distancing do you use in your relationships with others? To find out, turn to Table 10.1, and complete the evaluation.

Developing Good Relationships

How can you develop open, authentic relationships? The research on the subject is far from complete—and may never be. Still, we know a great deal about relationships, and what makes good ones happen. The two key ingredients are:

1. Valuing others, caring about them and showing it—without devaluing yourself. (See Chapter 4, Table 4.2.)
2. Being open, expressing honestly how you feel rather than playing roles you believe others expect you to play.

How to Be Open.   Now, just exactly how do you go about being open? Let's look at some examples. Suppose your business is bad, and you're worried. You meet a friend for lunch, and he asks, "How's everything?" For once, instead of the automatic response of, "Fine, just great," how about telling the truth? "To be honest, I'm worried sick. Business is terrible and I'm not sure what to do about it."

What will happen? For one thing, your friend will probably be surprised—and he may be delighted to discover a new and very human facet of your personality. He won't think you are weak for being worried. He's been worried plenty in his life, and he may be worried now, too. More likely, he'll think you're strong for being able to admit it. And he just may have an idea to help you that he would never have volunteered if you had responded, "Just great."

[4]Elwood N. Chapman, *Supervisor's Survival Kit* (Chicago, Ill.: Science Research Association, Inc., 1970), pp. 111–13.

Here's another example. Suppose you've made a mistake of some kind that creates a problem in your company. When confronted with it, instead of dodging, making excuses, or looking for a scapegoat, why not be open—say, "Yes, I'm responsible for that. I regret it, and I'm embarrassed, and I've certainly learned a valuable lesson."

What will happen? First, your honesty and sincerity will almost certainly defuse the anger in the situation. And again, you will show your humanness in admitting that you can and do make mistakes. Further, others will admire your courage for taking responsibility for your error. But, if you had made excuses, or tried to pin the blame elsewhere, they would distrust you and suspect you of far greater sins.

And, for a final example, let's say an anxious subordinate comes to you to report a mistake or tell you about a problem. Instead of leaping in with a decision or advice, take a moment to be open and human by sharing some similar experience: "I understand how you feel. When I first started, I made a customer so angry he tried to have me fired." Or, "I know that machine is tricky to run . . . I had a lot of trouble learning how to operate it myself."

This last example describes a technique called *self-disclosure*. It can go a long way toward opening an honest relationship and putting others at ease at the same time.

Now suppose you're up against a major misunderstanding with someone important to you. You understood one thing and they understood exactly the opposite. The way people usually handle this is through anger or attacking one another—and such behavior can often destroy a relationship. Instead, how about being honest and open: "Well, I don't know how we could have misunderstood each other so badly, but I suppose *how* it happened isn't important. I want to work this out and I hope you do. Let's see how we can do it."

In such situations, both of you think you are right—so actually, you may both be partially wrong. You've had a failure in communication. At this point, it's not important to pinpoint the *past* failure. What is important is to show you know you have honestly misunderstood one another and sincerely want to work things out.

How does all this relate to decision-making? When you learn to establish good relationships, you will greatly increase your input sources for making more effective decisions. At this point, we're ready to examine some proven ways to make decisions.

MAKING DECISIONS

Begin by basing your decisions, as consistently as possible, on the needs of the organization—not on your personal needs. Ask yourself, "What will help most to increase company sales or profits? Which choice will be best for the company or the department?"

Decisions that are based on your organization's needs will help you more personally in the long run—and help your organization more in the meantime. If you have good information and you base your decision on the needs of the organization, you can then use the scientific decision-making strategy.

Steps in Making Good Decisions

Here are the steps: First, *write down all the alternatives*. Say, for example, that you are trying to decide how to respond to a sudden incidence of poor service and performance from Ace Company, a major supplier. You might write alternatives like these:

A. Stay where I am and try to work it out.
B. Try a new supplier on a test basis.
C. Change suppliers immediately.

The second step is to *write down the advantages and disadvantages of each possible choice*. Specify as many pros and cons as you can think of. In deciding about your Ace Company, you might write these advantages for A, the first alternative—staying put and trying to work things out:

Ace knows our needs and our operation. If we can correct the problems, it will be easier and will require no disruption; less time, money, and effort will be involved.

After listing advantages for each alternative, list the disadvantages for each item on your list. For example:

It may be risky. I'm in the dark, because I don't really know what caused the sudden failures to perform, so Ace may have problems I can't work with. In the long run, it may cost more time, money, and effort.

The third step in making decisions is to *evaluate the pros and cons*. One way of doing this is to simply add up the score. Which alternative has the most advantages? That is the one you choose. And if some points on either side are more important than others, you can weigh them. Decide which pros and cons are most important to you, and give them a numerical value. For example, put them on a scale from 1 to 5, or 1 to 10, according to their value to your company or department. Add up the scores of the pros and cons, and you will get a total for each alternative.

In deciding about the supplier, you might rate the alternatives on a 5-point scale, this way:

Advantages: *They know our operation*—worth 3 points. *Easier and require no disruptions*—also 3 points. *Will require less time, effort, and money*—worth 5 points. That's a total of 11 for advantages.

Disadvantages: *It's risky*—that's 4 points. *I don't really know the source of the problem*—5 points. *It may cost more in the long run*— also 5 points. That's a total of 14 for the disadvantages.

Exercise

Your disadvantages outweigh the advantages—your choice is made. Table 10.2 contains a sample problem worked out for our example. Using this same format, evaluate the alternatives of a decision you are facing.

TABLE 10.2
Scientific Decision Making

Problem: Sudden rash of poor service from a major supplier.

Alternative	Advantages	Score	Disadvantages	Score
1. Stay where we are.	They know operation.	3	Risky.	4
	Easier.	3	Don't know source of problem.	5
	Less time, effort and money.	5	May cost more.	5
11−14= −3	TOTAL	11		14
2. Try new	Low risk	4	Coordination harder	4

TABLE 10.2 (Continued)

Alternative	Advantages	Score	Disadvantages	Score
Supplier on test basis.	Will locate source of problem.	5	May upset present supplier.	2
	Save some money.	2		
11−6= +5	TOTAL	11		6
3. Change immediately.	Save more mcney.	5	Transition takes a lot of time and effort.	4
	Conclusive action.	4	Disrupt long relationship.	2
	Change for change's sake.	2	Problem may not be present supplier's fault.	5
11−11= 0	TOTAL	11		11

Decision: Alternative #2

Once you have evaluated the alternatives, that's not the end of it. Make sure you really feel right about the course of action. Is there possibly another alternative you haven't considered?

Remember Your Feelings

Often, people (especially men) leave their feelings out of making decisions. Of course, the fact is that you cannot leave your feelings out of your decisions. They are always present, even if they are hidden. You can't think without involving your emotions, and you can't identify your emotions without thinking about them. So we can say that mind and body are one. There is no place where reason is involved without feelings or vice versa. A person is not split into different compartments; every human being is a unified whole—although many people don't act this way!

What does all this mean for you? In making decisions, especially major ones, it's important to consult *both* your logic and your emotions. In general, this is easier for women than for men, because most men have been trained to deny their emotions.

The male self-image is cool and rational, so many men don't tune in to their feelings—particularly in relation to business decisions. But the feelings are there nonetheless, and do effect the decisions. Become aware of what you're feeling. Often the best solution is the one you feel best about.

If you can't make a decision using the rational process, try examining each alternative you have listed, one at a time. Which one gives you the best gut-level feeling? If your instinct tells you that one choice *feels* right, that one may be best for you.

Think, too, about which alternative will leave you feeling best in the *long run*. If you are in doubt, talk over your feelings and your contemplated decision with someone you trust outside your department or company. Don't depend on people who only echo your aims and ideas. Go to people who are not personally involved, yet can comment objectively on your views. As you talk, you will often find the problem clarifying, and you will be surprised at the value of some of the innocent questions asked by your "sounding-board."

Finally, try to allow a little extra time for making important decisions. Too often managers—men and women alike—get caught in their own deadlines. Then something unexpected happens, and they are forced to make decisions they aren't ready to make.

Exercise

In my seminar for women managers, we use a mini-game adapted from the *Supervisor's Survival Kit* by Elwood N. Chapman.[5] Its primary purpose is to provide experience in making decisions under pressure. We take it a step further to learn which of the priorities will help you most as a woman/manager interested in getting ahead. The game is described in Table 10.3. After you complete it, compare your answers with the ones on page 206—these are the ones in your best interests as an up-and-coming manager.

TABLE 10.3
Priorities

PURPOSE: To provide experience in making decisions under pressure.

PROBLEM: You (the manager) left Monday morning for a one-week company-sponsored training program in supervisory leadership. Your department was turned over to Mrs. R., but she became ill and went home. It was then turned over to Mrs. K., but her mother became critically ill and she flew home. You were called two hours ago and asked to return on an

[5]Ibid.

TABLE 10.3 (Continued)

emergency basis. You arrived five minutes ago. The time is 1:00 P.M. The day is Friday. As you walk into your office, you face ten critical problems.

PROCEDURE: These problems are listed below. Please read, evaluate, and give a priority number to each of these ten problems. In other words, decide which problem you should handle first, second, third, and so forth. You have only 5 minutes to do this.

Set a timer for five minutes and read all ten problems. Then assign the priority numbers. If you have not finished in 5 minutes, you lose the game.

PRIORITIES COMPARISON

	Your Priority Assignment	
A.	( )	You have received a report from Miss Personnel that Ms. L. is looking for another job outside the company. She wants you to talk to her. You figure this would take you 15 minutes.
B.	( )	Mr. Big has left word that he wants to see you in his office immediately upon your return. Anticipated time: 60 minutes.
C.	( )	You have some very important-looking unopened mail (both company and personal) on your desk. Time: 10 minutes.
D.	( )	Your telephone is ringing.
E.	( )	A piece of equipment has broken down, halting all production in your department. You are the only one who can fix it. Anticipated time: 30 minutes.
F.	( )	A very attractive man is seated outside your office waiting to see you. Time: 10 minutes.
G.	( )	You have an urgent written notice in front of you to call a Los Angeles operator. Both your mother and the company headquarters are located in Los Angeles. Time: 10 minutes.
H.	( )	Mr. Demanding has sent word he wants to see you and has asked that you return his call as soon as possible. Time: 10 minutes.
I.	( )	Miss Q. is in the women's lounge and says she's sick. She wants your permission to go home. It will take about 15 minutes to get the facts and make a decision.

TABLE 10.3 (Continued)

J.	( )	In order to get to your office by 1:00 P.M., you had to miss lunch. You are very hungry, but you figure it will take 30 minutes to get something substantial to eat.

From *Supervisor's Survival Kit* by Elwood N. Chapman. © 1970 Science Research Associates, Inc. Reprinted by permission of the publisher.

Desirable Rank-Ordering

The general consensus in most seminars is that the following rank-ordering s in a woman manager's best interests:

A.	#4	This is high because Ms. L. may be a key employee and the discussion will only take 15 minutes.
B.	#1	Mr. Big is the president. He also has a much bigger picture of the company. Just as important, you don't want to miss any opportunities to gain access to the top.
C.	#5	It's waited all week; it can wait a few more hours.
D.	#7	Low priority. Let your secretary answer and screen.
E.	#2	Get production moving.
F.	#9	Usually, game-players decide to put this and J (lunch) together.
G.	#3	High priority—either way, headquarters or mother, you'll work better if anxiety is eased.
H.	#8	Low priority. He's probably an every-day nuisance.
I.	#6	If Miss Q. were really sick she'd have gone home. It may seem inhumane, but this is not high-priority.
J.	#10	Either send out for a sandwich and eat it while you do E and G, or wait and go with F.

Use Your Subconscious

If you try reasoning out a solution, consulting your feelings, *and* talking things over with someone you trust and you still can't make a decision, try putting the power of your subconscious mind to work.

Few people are even aware of the great power of their subconscious. But they may often have experienced having the solution to a knotty problem seem to just "pop" into their heads. They don't realize that their subconscious minds have done the work. Often, if you try to tell people to use their subconscious in decision-making, they react with derision or at least surprise.

It's understandable that some people feel this way—not many people really know how the brains works. In a series of studies of patients undergoing brain surgery, noted Canadian brain surgeon W. Penfield, found that the human brain stores every single thing that has ever happened to you, from the day of your birth. Most of this experience has been long forgotten by your conscious mind—but it is possible to use your subconscious to help you in decision-making. If you learn to put your subconscious mind to work on your problems, you will harness considerable power. But how is this done?

First, make sure your problem is written down, along with the pros and cons of each alternative, as you did earlier. Second, if you can't solve the problem consciously, pretend your subconscious mind is a subordinate; give it an assignment and deadline: "This is my problem. I'd like an answer by Thursday morning."

Third, put the problem out of your conscious mind. Don't think about it at all. This is extremely important, because just as two people can't work in a crowded space, your subconscious mind won't work on a problem if your conscious mind is preoccupied with it. So forget about it for a while. If you don't worry about it, the answer will come to you.

How will you know if you have the answer? You will not hear mysterious "voices." The solution to the problem will just *come* to you. It will "feel" like the *right* answer. You will also want to get right back to the problem and put that answer to work at once.

Many creative people do their best work by putting their subconscious mind to work. You've probably heard that many top executives keep a pencil and pad on their night table—so that when their subconscious wakes them with an idea or a solution, they can write it down immediately. And many writers put a demanding piece of creative writing on what they call "the back burner"—and loaf for a few days. Then out of the blue, they sit down and write the piece in a few hours. If you ask them how they did it, they'll say: "Nothing to it. It really wrote itself."

In summary, when you face a decision, *try to find the answer systematically*. If that doesn't do it, *consult your feelings,* particularly the net emotional effect of each alternative. And if you're really stuck, *put the power of your subconscious mind to work.*

When you've made your choice, stay flexible. Don't feel you're married to one course of action. If events show that your decision was wrong, be free to admit it and take another course. Always consider that there may be another alternative you haven't thought of.

Assertiveness Training

People often fail as executives because they actually fear making decisions. This fear usually stems from an internal conflict over the desire to be courageous and the fear of failure. So they twist and turn; they may become mentally paralyzed and withdraw from the decision-making process completely. Others hate to say no, or can't face up to subordinates.

You can conquer this problem or lack of confidence with a technique psychologists call assertive training.

The key to assertive training is learning new behavior in small steps. You practice asserting yourself in unimportant or nonthreatening situations in order to learn to be assertive in more threatening ones. If you find this difficult, reward yourself along the way with your favorite activities or with token points toward something material you want—a new tennis racquet, a camera, massage, or the like. When you collect enough points, you get your reward.

Use Fantasy.   The easiest way to begin is to fantasize. Sit back and relax. Imagine a situation in which you would like to be more confident. Picture the situation and the person clearly, with as many details as possible. Imagine what the other person says, and how you respond confidently. Then picture the other person agreeing with you. If you practice imagining you can be confident in these situations, it will help you be more confident when they occur in real life.

Rehearse.   Once you have imagined yourself as being more assertive, stand in front of a mirror and pretend you are in a tough decision-making situation. Imagine, for example, that you have been instructed to fire two of your staff because of overall company cutbacks. Pretend you are meeting with your superior in an attempt to decide which two you will terminate. Practice what you will say. Tape-record it, if possible. Watch your facial expressions and general attitude. Are you acting confident and relaxed?

Practice with Minor Decisions.   Next, apply this new confidence to making minor decisions in real life. Take it in small steps, and remember, you don't need to be popular—you need to make the right decisions for the company. This helps you get matters away from the personal level.

Confront the Real Situation.   The last step in assertiveness training is to confront the situation, people, and decisions which you find most difficult. For example, suppose declining sales and profits make it apparent you must cut at least 25 percent of your operating budget. This is a difficult decision because it means letting staff go, or at best, changing their jobs within the company. Effecting a decision like this takes a lot of courage. It means being willing to be Ms. Company, to do the tough thing, make the unpopular decision, and stand alone for a while. If you practice assertiveness training and apply it to your experience in business, you will gradually feel equal to almost all of the problems you must face.

Courage, after all, comes from experience, and is a quality any determined woman can develop.

11
Increasing
Your
Effectiveness

In the last chapter, we examined some strategies for making more effective decisions. In this chapter, we'll examine some ways to further increase your effectiveness as a manager—specifically, by (1) learning to organize your own time better, and (2) learning to "get others to do the work."

TIME

Stop for a moment and think about the uniqueness of *time*. It is the one resource that is truly and strictly limited. Of all the major resources—money, commodities, knowledge, people—only time is irreplaceable. It is perishable; it cannot be stored. Yesterday's time is gone forever and cannot be regained. And there is no substitute for it.

Furthermore, everything requires time. There is nothing you can *do*—work, rest, or play—that does not use time.

In my experience, the hallmark of truly effective executives is the way they protect and invest their time. But unfortunately, most people do not manage time well.

There are two basic methods of successfully managing time:

1. Organizing your own time
2. Delegating to others

The first method involves knowing how you spend your time now, eliminating time-wasters, and consolidating your available time into working blocks. The second method involves getting others to "take the monkey off your back." Let's look at each method in detail.

ORGANIZING YOUR TIME

To organize time, first you need to know how you spend it. Few executives really know where their time goes. If you ask them to make a "time pie" (a graphic record of their time investments) and then record what they really do with their time, you will have two completely different pictures.

What about you? Do you know how you spend your time? If you don't keep a daily or weekly "time log" of some kind, the answer is probably "no." Let's see.

Make a "Time Pie"

Exercise

Draw a large circle or pie on a piece of paper. Divide it into sixteen segments and fill in each slice with half-hour time slices representing your average day—i.e., 9:00 A.M. to 9:30 A.M., 9:30 A.M. to 10:00 A.M., and so on. Now, in each slice, fill in what you did yesterday, its purpose, and whether or not you accomplished your purpose.

Now add up the slices you spend on different activities: developing subordinates, thinking, planning, writing reports, attending meetings, handling crises, solving people and technical problems, and so forth.

Then, for the next six weeks, keep a daily record of what you really do and how much time you spend on each activity. At the end of the six weeks, summarize your log, total the hours for each activity, and compare it to the first version which you did from memory. I guarantee that if you do this exercise you will rapidly change the way you protect and invest your time.

Note: This is not a one-time exercise. Do it on a regular schedule—at least twice a year. You will almost always find you have drifted back into wasting your time on unimportant or unnecessary trivia.

Find Out How You Waste Time

The next step in organizing your time is to find the ways you or others waste your time. Begin by asking yourself these questions about each item on your time log:

1. Is this an activity that others can do, should do, or can be trained to do?

If you answer "yes" to this question for any activity, then it is your responsibility as a manager to delegate these jobs to your subordinates.

2. Does this activity really need to be done at all? What would happen if it didn't get done?

If your answers are negative, obviously you have to stop doing it. It is mind-boggling to find how many things busy people are doing that simply are not needed. For example, for years I didn't trust the computer printouts of sales and marketing figures. So, before the figures went to the computer, I had people hand-post the information for me and then I would spend at least an hour or two every day doing my own calculations. When the computer printouts came in weekly, I would spend another few hours checking them against *my* records and gleefully pounce on any "errors" the computer made. This, in turn, led to more time spent tracking down the discrepancies—it also led to disagreements, distrust, and sometimes dyspepsia. Lucky for me, it was my own company. Anywhere else I would have been severely criticized. But managers—and subordinates—do spend precious time on endless tasks that don't contribute a thing to getting the real job done. To the best of your ability, you need to find these time-wasters and eliminate them.

3. Is this job urgent or important? What would happen if you put it off till later?

Silber and Sherman point out that the urgent is seldom important and the important seldom urgent.[1] And the corollary of this statement is that, as a manager, you delegate the urgent and keep the important. Your job as a manager is to do the important work of setting priorities, making plans and decisions, developing people, and using your skills to get the job done. Effective (and promotable) managers don't just "mind the store." Therefore, when an urgent request comes in, give it to the most qualified person on your staff to take care of.

---

[1]Mark B. Silber and V. Clayton Sherman, *Managerial Performance and Promotability: The Making of an Executive* (New York: American Management Assn., Inc., 1974).

If a task is neither urgent nor important, then it is something that can be done later, in slack time—and done by somebody other than you.

4. Can someone else do this job as well as, or better than, you?

This involves your ego, and it's not always easy to admit that someone else can do a job as well as or better than you can (more on ego problems in this chapter later). Still, no matter why you are reluctant to delegate, your first concern is *results:* achieving your job objectives and developing people. If you hang on to tasks that others can do you are creating barriers to your own advancement.

5. Finally, what are you doing that wastes other people's time?

You may waste others' time in one of two ways:

a. Using an inefficient working style
b. Being a bottleneck

I have a partner who is now in danger of his life for the way he wastes other people's time. He's my husband and here is his trick: Each and every program, workshop leader's guide, training instrument, etc., we develop gets set in type (at considerable cost). We then print from this master artwork as needed. When we *customize* something for a client, the procedure is to make a Xerox copy of the master and make revisions on the copy. Not Allen Cannie. He goes into the master art and makes his corrections on *it!* (Some of these files are 200–300 pages long and he pulls out 50 or 60 pages.) His defense is that he saves time because we only set the corrections! He simply cannot comprehend that he is creating monstrous headaches and wasting enormous amounts of time by destroying finished sets of finished art.

In fact, I think he really does know he's making unnecessary extra work. It's just easier for him. He is doing productive work but at a major waste of other people's time. What about you?

Inefficient Working Style.   Are you wasting other people's time simply because of the way you do your own work? There is only one way to find out. Ask your people, sincerely, "What do I do that wastes your time without contributing to your development?" This isn't easy, of course, but you need this feedback. If you have built trusting relationships with your subordinates, you will get the truth. And it will help you, and them, be more effective.

Being a Bottleneck.   A second way you waste time is to be the bottleneck: work can't go forward because it needs your input, approval, or whatever. You get behind and perhaps a whole department sits idle waiting for you to "get to it." Or you may have too many people waiting to ask you questions because you are the only one who knows the answer. If people can't get to see you for a few days, they must wait before they can go ahead.

If this happens in your department, it's a good sign you have not developed your people. Somehow, in some way, you need to learn that you are not the only one who can do most of the activities you spend time on. *You* learned them—others can learn them, too.

It is important to remember that *everyone* is replaceable and everyone *is* replaced. Remind yourself of this truth the next time you feel that no one else can be trained to do something you are hanging onto.

Classic Time-Wasters.   Once you have answered these questions, you will have some control over your own time-wasting activities. Then take a look at the classic time-wasters: the recurrent crisis, too many human relations problems, and "meeting-itis."

Any crisis that repeats itself more than twice is one that should not occur again. Such crises indicate sloppy or lazy management. They *can* be foreseen; therefore, they can be prevented by establishing step-by-step procedures or routines.

In his book *The Effective Executive*, Drucker notes that a well-managed plant or organization is quiet and "dull." Nothing dramatic or heroic happens, no fires need to be put out, or no mopping up is necessary. All the crises have been anticipated and have been converted to routines.[2]

Another classic time and resource-waster results from having too many human relations problems. These problems may be a result of the job climate. As we saw in an earlier chapter, both the formal and informal climates create these problems by having too much, or not enough, structure and through inadequate systems of challenge, communication, feedback, and reward. People working in these climates are either resentful, angry, and frustrated or lazy, unproductive, and disloyal. And, as you've seen, these are all elements you control through your own leadership style.

"Meeting-itis" is the final classic time-waster—and most large and medium-sized companies are guilty of having too many meetings.

[2]Peter Drucker, *The Effective Executive* (New York: Harper & Row, 1967).

What is the purpose of a meeting? The true purpose of a meeting is to put heads together to solve a problem, because one person doesn't have the knowledge or experience required to do it alone. That's OK, because in a well-managed organization these meetings are the exception.

But most meetings are *not* held for this purpose. Rather, they are held to convey information that may already be known or decisions that have already been made (and both of these can be done more effectively by memos); or to display the power of the person who calls the meeting. Such meetings are usually a complete waste of time; you can't meet and work at the same time.

My own way of handling excessive meetings is to be too busy—and ask for a verbal report from someone who attends. In a word, the report on "what happened" at the so-and-so meeting is, as a rule, "nothing."

Consolidating Discretionary Time

This brings us to the third step in organizing your time: consolidating discretionary time.

The first thing you will learn from studying your time log is that no matter how strictly you protect your day, you still aren't going to have excessive amounts of time in which to do your really important tasks. No matter how well-disciplined you may be, a lot of your time will be spent on things that contribute little, if anything, to productivity. People drop in, customers call for help or favors, there are long luncheons and ceremonial functions, you must entertain clients, attend meetings, and make decisions. In addition, as a manager you work with a unique resource: people. And people are time-consumers as well as time-wasters.

All of this comes down to your own fractured and constantly interrupted daily time pie. Yet most of your tasks require fairly large chunks of time. For example, to plan for a future activity, you may need a minimum of six to eight hours. To try to do this planning in fifteen- or twenty-minute segments over several weeks isn't very effective. And this applies to almost all of your important tasks. You need large chunks of time. How can you get this time? By consolidating the time which your time log shows is under your control.

There are many ways of consolidating time into six- or eight-hour blocks. Here are some possibilities:

1. Work at home either one day a week or two mornings a week.

2. Schedule all meetings, travel, interviews, etc., on certain days—say Monday and Friday—and leave the other days unscheduled. Block out time each day for your own tasks and do not permit any interruptions.

3. Work according to your "inner time clock"—that period each day when you operate at your peak performance. This time should be saved for your most difficult tasks and for just plain thinking. If you have two "prime-time" periods a day, save both of them for your own work. For example, I have two periods on my inner time clock when I work best and think clearest. One is between 2 A.M. and 4 A.M. (unfortunately). I wake every day and think for two hours. Sometimes I review, other times I wake with creative ideas (I write them down). Still other times I wrestle with knotty problems. Whatever, this is a very productive time for me. My next peak time is between 11 A.M. and 3 P.M. This is when I write. I close everything else out except emergencies, and I have learned to do this, no matter what. When my children were growing up I used to work at home three days a week—to do my creative writing. I had an office and a sign for the door which I put up between 11 A.M. and 3 P.M. It read "Do not enter unless bleeding profusely from the head." My children respected this without question. And, more importantly, it banned the household help who, otherwise, would have been interrupting me about such "burning" issues as "two quarts of milk or three?"

Delegating

Once you have your own time well organized, your next step is to delegate. As I said in an earlier chapter, delegating does not mean that you do it and others help you, or that others do it and you peer over their shoulders. It means that other people do the job and you stay responsible for it. Someone once wrote, "Executive ability is deciding quickly and getting somebody else to do the work."

The single most important reason for delegating responsibilities to others is to increase your available time to do your own important work. Naturally, a key side benefit is that you also develop your people. This, in turn, increases the effectiveness of your operation and enhances your chances for rising in the business. But the critical issue here is your time.

You have to learn to delegate everything you need not do personally.

If you study your time log, you will soon see that there is seldom time to do the things that are important—things you want to do, and are committed to do. The only way you will have half a chance to do these important tasks is to push off onto others things you don't need to do personally.

Of course, most managers know this—in fact, they've given the "delegating" sermon often enough themselves to subordinates. But despite all the preaching about delegating, not many managers follow their own advice.

There are probably hundreds of reasons for this state of affairs—but in my view, the three key barriers to delegating concern ego needs:

1. *Wanting to be wanted.* Most people like to be helpful. But too often, helping others really turns out to be destructive generosity. Doing things for others that they can do for themselves doesn't really help them—and it denies people the personal responsibility and satisfaction they are seeking.

2. *Desire to stay in control.* This is typically more of a problem with men than women. In fact, one of the hardest things to teach men managers is to stop overcontrolling. No one can control everything. And when a manager tries to control everything, his or her workers lose out—because they don't get trained for more responsibility.

3. *Anxiety over the progress of junior employees.* When people reach responsible jobs, they are usually middle-aged, with young subordinates under them. Many of these managers fear being overtaken by employees who have brains, vigor, and enthusiasm. So to ease their anxieties over being replaced, they won't turn over responsibilities to these younger staff members.

OTHER WAYS TO INCREASE YOUR EFFECTIVENESS

After you have learned to organize your time and delegate responsibilities, will your problems be over? Certainly not—there are many other miscellaneous areas in which you can learn to increase your effectiveness—to function at your best—as a woman manager in a traditionally male environment.

Dealing with Nervousness

One problem you may have as a woman manager is that you may get nervous in meetings . . . especially meetings with senior managers. Of course, when you're nervous, you can't think too well. So you may blurt out something stupid or critical. Or your tongue may freeze when someone directs a question at you.

Every pipe-smoking man has a ready solution for such situations. He can gain from 30 seconds to 3 minutes going through the puffing, tapping, scraping, and refilling pipe rituals. *You can clean your glasses.* That's right. Take them off. Inspect them against the light. Reach for a tissue (even better, use the hem of your skirt) and clean them carefully while you gain your composure. Don't hurry. It's more important that you think straight and say the right thing, even if you have to make people wait. You don't wear glasses? Get a pair.

Raises

Another special problem you may have as a woman manager may occur when you want more money. I personally feel that it's a serious mistake to ask for a raise. Most men don't want to give it to you, and asking for it makes you seem petty and greedy. Instead, ask for a promotion or for more responsibility—that involves a whole different issue. You will look motivated and ambitious—and this will surprise and delight most men. Besides, if you get the promotion, the money will follow.

Dealing with Romantic Advances

Next, there is the matter of romantic or sexual advances. This is not a problem for many women. They project an attitude of "hands off" and men can usually read this message. But in the event you have a problem, the best thing to do is to take the responsibility for the situation by saying "I don't know what I've done to let you think I was inviting this. I'm sorry. I didn't mean to mislead you." This saves a man's ego, and usually the relationship.

Unfortunately, successful women are often suspected of having "slept her way to the top." Maybe there are women who have succeeded through sex but I don't know any of them. If you want to try it, go ahead. But the word from here is it will do you more harm than good. When the romance is over, you may be an embarrassment to be gotten rid of.

I could write a whole book on some of the crazy situations I've encountered . . . in huge private offices, in cozy restaurants, at conventions. And if I had slept with all the men I've been accused of sleeping with, I wouldn't have had time for anything else. However, the point I want to make is that women are often the target for men who are trying to prove their masculinity. But once these men win the prize, they need another challenge. So try not to be swept away by romantic, and usually attractive men. Don't be a victim.

Entertaining Customers

Despite the progress made on the women's liberation front, the great majority of men are still uptight chauvinists when it comes to women picking up the tab for lunch or dinner.

There is no sense whatsoever in making an issue of this, because there are so many easy ways around it. For instance, you can:

1. Join a private club and take your guests there to wine and dine. Only you can sign.
2. Establish yourself at one restaurant and have it bill you. Arrange ahead for no check to be presented.
3. If you can't manage either of the above, emphasize the fact that it's on the company and is not your money. Or say your company wants you to take care of these expenses.

Whatever you do, don't make a big issue over it. If a man's ego is really threatened—and you'll know when it is—let him pick up the check.

One more item on entertaining (or being entertained) concerns having drinks. If your customer orders a drink and you don't want one, don't have one! You can order a nonalcoholic drink. *Don't* say virtuously, "I don't drink."

Hotel Rooms

If you travel, chances are that you've already found that you don't always get the choice rooms. Hotel clerks are usually men, and they have to stick somebody with the smallest, oldest, noisiest rooms they have—some of them figure a woman won't complain (and unfortunately, they may be right much of the time!).

If you go to a particular city often, stay at the same hotel every time. Let the hotel know that you want the corporation rate (25 to 30 percent off) and you want a quiet room.

If you are an occasional traveler, let the room clerk know your wishes about a room. If you don't like what they give you, tell the bellhop "This won't do." He's looking for a tip, so he makes the call to the front desk to get you something you want.

Traveling with Male Colleagues

Don't be available any more than the job demands. Clear ahead what is expected of you in the evenings. If you're not working or entertaining a customer, make plans for yourself. Don't expect to be entertained—and don't entertain! Also, don't explain. Just say you have other plans.

Dining Alone

If you travel, you are going to eat alone often. Many women dread this and wind up ordering food in their rooms. There's nothing wrong with this if you're more comfortable this way. A good trick is to order breakfast in your room the night before, to avoid the morning crush.

But you can miss a lot in a new city if you don't try a few good restaurants. So make a reservation for one and follow the same principle about your table as for hotel rooms. If you don't like the table, don't even sit down. Just say, "This won't do."

Credit

This is not the problem it once was. Today women are having less trouble establishing credit on their own. If a bank or store gives you a problem, just let them know you're aware of your rights. It won't take long to set things right.

Marriage

Now you get a nice bonus. All the skills you have learned in this book apply to your marriage—or to any relationship, for that matter. You need to communicate, and to know what makes the other person tick, and how to handle conflicts. You need to know how to negotiate and persuade, and how to make decisions. You need to know how to make contracts, and allocate your time, and even delegate! In short, the same skills you need as a good manager will help you be a good marriage partner—and parent.

But if you have children, or are planning on having them, be prepared to sacrifice time in your career—and go to work for a company that understands when you have a sick child you can't really do good work. You might as well be home.

Even better, if you have or want to have children, start your own business—alone or with a partner. The Small Business Administration has millions of dollars appropriated to help women and other disadvantaged groups go into their own businesses. They'll lend you money and in most cities, have low-cost or free training programs to help you succeed.

Getting and Decorating an Office

This is a sore spot with me. Men tend to take the best offices for themselves and think you either don't need or don't want one.

The only way to get what you want is to speak up: say what you want! Don't take it for granted that if you get a promotion, you'll get a better office. Keep in mind the procedure for getting good hotel rooms and good tables in restaurants. If you are given an office that is not comparable to what the male managers have, don't take it. Smile sweetly and say, "This won't do at all. I'd be very unhappy (uncomfortable, unproductive, un-anything) with this. I want . . ."

Once you get the office, make it distinctly your own by the way you decorate it. Make it your sanctuary, your turf, your power base. Anyone coming into your personal, private preserve is going to be on *your* ground. *You'll* have the advantage. That is just what you want.

Handling Resentment

The higher up you go, the more resentment and jealousy you'll encounter—from both men and women. Some people have a lot of hangups about working for a woman and create a lot of problems. This may never happen to you. I hope it doesn't. But if it does, whatever else you do, don't get defensive. Use the skills you have learned in this book, and always keep your focus on performance and achieving goals.

Lifelong Growth

Keep on growing. There is no limit to how much you can grow and learn and do—only *you* determine that. Be an insatiable reader—not one book a week, but two or three. Everything the world knows about every subject is in books. A single book often provides the sum total of an author's lifetime of knowledge and experience. Read three books a week and you gain the know-how of three lifetimes! Think of it.

You can take college courses if you want, but you'll be paying a lot of money for one professor and two or three textbooks per semester. If you read everything you can find on subjects and skills you need to help you grow, you will make huge leaps in knowledge and understanding—which you can then translate into behavior.

I can't emphasize enough the importance of learning effective behavioral skills in order to be a really good manager. You can have an IQ of 170, a string of degrees, great technical or professional skill. But these aren't worth a nickel if you don't behave in the ways—i.e., *do the things*—necessary to have a successful career. I have tried to tell you as many of the behaviors I know that can help you do this. Now, for a final assignment, go on out there and do it!

Index

Allport, Gordon, *Becoming: Basic Consid-
    erations for a Psychology of Personal-
    ity,* 3–4
Argyris, Chris, 47, 58
assertiveness training, 208–9
Atkinson, John W., 47, 58
attending, 111–13, 116, 118
    exercises, 113
authority, 29, 61
    See also Leadership styles

behavior:
    coping, 17–22, 25, 26, 31
    defensive, 16–22, 25, 26, 29–31, 76, 153
    learned, 30
    self-defeating, 80–86
behavior modification, 24–25, 30, 31,
    208–9
Berne, Eric, 113; *What Do You Do After You
    Say Hello?,* 80–83
Bertalanffy, Ludwig von, *General System
    Theory,* 12–14
body language, 68, 95, 98–99, 109, 112–13
Booker, Gene, 9

Calero, Henry, 99–100
case studies:
    behavioral impact on others, 32–33
    conflicts, 165–66
    criticism, handling of, 32–33
    defensive vs. coping behavior, 17–18
    motivation, 72–74
    promotion problems, 155–56, 159–60,
        161
    responsibility acceptance, 23, 24
    threatening questions, 133
    time wasting, 214
Chapman, Elwood N., *Supervisor's Survival
    Kit,* 204–6

communication, communication problems,
    43, 93–107
    assumptions, 102, 107, 110, 143–44
    "but" messages, 106
    contracting, 147–50
    exercises, 95, 96–98, 99, 104, 140–43,
        145–47, 149–50
    eye contact in, 112
    hidden expectations, 102–3, 107
    incomplete messages, 101–3
    irresponsible messages, 104–6, 107
    judging messages, 100–101
    kidding, 95–96, 98, 107, 118
    meta-talk messages, 99–100
    mixed messages, 94–95, 109
    nonverbal, 68, 95, 98–99, 109
    questions as, 132–43
    sarcasm, 94, 95–96, 98–99, 107
    "should" messages, 30, 103–4
    tentative phrases in, 143–47
    See also Attending; Listening; Reflection;
        Stroking
competition, competitiveness, 7, 33, 153, 154
conflicts, conflict management, 69, 153–70
    case studies, 155–56, 159–60, 161,
        165–66
    confrontation of, 153–54, 180–81, 187
    constructive confrontation, 158–65, 168
    diplomatic disagreement, 156–58
    exercises, 157–58, 162–64, 168–70
    interpersonal, 155–70
    sexual games and, 167–70
    among subordinates, 153–55
    as woman, 155–56, 159–60, 161, 166–70
contracting, 147–50, 179
    exercises, 149–50
coping behavior, 17–19, 26, 31
    exercises, 19–22, 25
credit, credit cards, 222

criticism, 7, 32–33, 34–36
of subordinates, 65
See also Fogging
customer entertainment, 220

decision-making, 43, 61, 85–86, 89–90,
110, 190–209
distancing in, 195–97
exercises, 202–3, 204–6
strategies in, 201–9
subconscious in, 206–8
women's role in organization and, 190–95
defensive behavior, 16–18, 26, 76, 153
avoidance of, 29–31
exercises, 19–22, 25
delegating, 62–63, 89, 211, 212, 213–14,
217–18
barriers to, 218
disapproval. *See* Criticism
distancing, 195–97
dress codes, 60–61, 79
Drucker, Peter H., 172
Effective Executive, The, 215
*Management Tasks, Responsibilities,
Practices*, 185–86
Dyer, Wayne, *Your Erroneous Zones*, 35–36
Dynamic Systems Theory, 12–14

empathy, as management skill, 40–41
exercises and quizzes:
attending, 113
career commitment, 9–10
communication, 95, 96–98, 99, 104
conflict and conflict management, 157–
58, 162–64
contracting, 149–50
coping vs. defending, 19–22, 25
decision-making, 202–3
distancing, 195–96
end result, 22, 25
fogging, 38–40
goals, 176–77
job satisfaction, 77
leadership styles, 48–52
listening, 110
management by objectives, 176–77
priorities, 204–6
questions, 140–43
respecting subordinates, 85
sexual game-playing, 168–70
tentative phrases, 145–47
time use, 212–13
Who am I?, 8

Fayol, Henri, *General and Industrial Management*, 41
feedback, 55, 61, 65, 66–68, 87, 181–82
feelings, control of, 24–25, 32–33, 155,
162, 167, 168, 208, 223

flexibility (management skill), 7, 33, 43, 60,
61
fogging (communication technique), 36–38
exercises, 38–40

Given, William B., *How to Manage People*,
62–63
goals, 5, 8, 9
exercises, 9–10, 14–16, 176–77
fuzziness of, 32, 175–78, 181
See also Management by objectives

Halpin, A.W., 68
Harvard Business Review management
study, 198–99
Henning, Margaret and Jardim, Anne, *Man-
agerial Woman, The*, 34
Hershey, Lenore, 29
Herzberg, Frederick:
Motivation to Work, The, 76–78
Work and the Nature of Man, 76–78
Horowitz, R. N., 47

Jardim, Anne, 34

Killian, Ray, *Human Resource Management: An ROI Approach*, 90–91, 93
Korda, Michael, *Power! How to Get It, How
to Use It*, 194

leadership styles, 47–70
exercises, 48–52
formal, 47, 48, 53
high achievement, 47, 60–70, 153,
154–55
informal, 47, 48, 53
negative, 55–56
overstructuring in, 59–61
positive, 56–57
structure and control in, 58–61
underlying assumptions and, 53–54
Levinson, Harry, "Appraisal of *What* Performance?" 183–84
life scripts, 80–83
Likert, Rensis, 47, 58, 68
listening, as management skill, 38, 40,
109–10, 118, 119, 129
exercises, 110
See also Attending; Communication and
communication problems; Reflection

McClelland, David C., 47, 87
McGregor, Douglas, 47, 58, 68, 79, 195
Human Side of Enterprise, The, 53–54
Mager, Robert, *Goal Analysis*, 175
management by objectives (MBO), 172–88
case studies, 179–80
cautions about, 188
effectiveness of, 173–74, 185–86

management by objectives (MBO) *(cont'd.)*
  feedback in, 174, 181–82
  goals in, 174–81, 183–87
  subordinates in, 173–75, 178–81, 186–87
management functions and roles, 2, 29,
  41–45, 174–75, 181, 185–86, 213.
  See also specific topics
management skills and techniques:
  communicating, 43, 93–107
  competitiveness, 7, 33, 153, 154
  criticism, handling of, 7, 32–33, 34–36
  delegating, 62–63, 89, 211, 212, 213–14,
    217–18
  empathy, 40–41
  flexibility, 7, 33, 43, 60, 61
  listening, 38, 40, 109–10, 118, 119, 129
  motivation, 52, 54–55, 59, 61–70, 72–74,
    77–80
  risk-taking, 7, 33–34, 43, 47, 56, 69–70,
    198–99
  stretching, 63–64
  valuing and respecting others, 30, 31, 40,
    55–57, 68, 70, 83–86, 90, 111, 116–17
marriage, 9–10, 222
Maslow, Abraham, 84
  "Theory of Human Motivation, A,"
    74–76, 77, 78
meetings, as time-wasters, 215–16
men, problems with:
  promotions, 155–56, 159–60, 161
  role-playing games, 168–70
  romantic/sexual, 219–20
mentors, 15, 155, 191
meta-talk, 99–100
  downers, 100
  foreboders, 100
  softeners, 99–100
Mintzberg, Henry, "Manager's Job:
  Folklore and Fact, The," 41–43
motivation, 52, 54–55, 59, 61–70, 72–74,
  77–80
Murray, Henry A., *Explorations in Personality,* 86–87

needs, need satisfaction, 72–91
  achievement, 87, 89
  affiliation, 87–88, 89
  dominance, 88–89
  hierarchy of, 74–76
  personality, 86–87
  See also specific needs
Nierenberg, Gerald and Calero, Henry,
  Meta-Talk, 99–100
note-taking, 110

office politics, 11, 59, 60, 154, 166, 183,
  190–95
office space, 222–23

organizational structure:
  informal, 7, 9, 11–14
  See also Leadership styles; Management
  skills and techniques

Penfield, W., 207
performance standards and appraisal, 64–65,
  181–84, 186–87
  See also Management by objectives
Perls, Fritz, 112
problem-solving. *See* Decision-making
projection (defense mechanism), 16
promotions, promotability, 33, 155–56,
  159–60, 161, 219

questions, 132–43
  to avoid, 136–39, 140
  dishonest, 139
  exercises, 140–43
  honest, 139
  leading, 139
  mixed-message, 138–39
  open, 134–36, 180, 181
  safe, 134–36
  statements substituted for, 137–38,
    139–40
  threatening, 31, 118, 132–34, 135, 140
  unfinished, 136
  "why," 31, 118, 132–34, 140
quizzes. *See* Exercises and quizzes

recognition, 73, 74, 79
reflection, 118–30
  of content, 121, 126
  exercises, 121, 122–29
  of feeling, 121, 123–26
  uses of, 128–30, 133–34, 155, 180
relationships (business), 190–200
  barriers in, 196–98
  exercises, 195–96
responsibility:
  acceptance of, 23–24, 26, 30, 31, 200
  of subordinates, 61–64, 79, 87, 162
rewards, 65–68, 79, 149, 166, 183
risk-taking, 7, 33–34, 43, 47, 56, 69–70,
  198–99
Rogers, Carl, *Client-Centered Therapy,* 119
role-playing, 113, 140, 168–70
Rutherberg, Louis, 194

salaries and fringe benefits, as motivators,
  73, 77, 78, 83–84
  raises, 219
self-actualization, 75, 76
self-concept, and management, 3–6, 155
  approval and, 35–36
  body self and, 3–4
  defensive behavior and, 16–19
  early training and, 6–7

self-concept, and management *(cont'd.)*
  influence of others on, 4–5, 6–8, 9, 11
  parental feedback and, 4, 7
  phony roles in, 7, 8
  values and goals in, 5, 8–9
self-disclosure (management technique), 200
selfishness, constructive, 31
self-respect, 30
sexual advances, 219–20
Sherman, V. Clayton, 11, 187, 213
"should's," 30, 103–4
Silber, Mark B. and Sherman, V. Clayton, *Managerial Performance and Promotability: The Making of an Executive,* 11, 187, 213
Sirota, David, 79
Smith, Manuel J., *When I Say No, I Feel Guilty,* 36–37
stretching (management technique), 63–64
stroking, 113–18
  conditional, 114–15, 116
  of group, 116
  influence on behavior of, 115–16
  negative, 114
  positive, 114
  sincerity of, 116–18
  unconditional, 114, 116

subordinates, 43, 45
  appraisal of manager by, 186–87, 214
  conflict resolution with, 153–55
  goals for, 44, 47, 61
  in management by objectives, 173–75, 178–81
  manager's interest in, 29, 86
  with problems, 83–86, 90, 111, 116–17
  See also Leadership styles

tentative phrases, 143–47
  exercises, 145–47
time-planning, 211–17
  exercises, 212–14, 216
travel (business), 221–22

valuing:
  of others, 30, 31, 40, 55–57, 68, 70, 83–86, 90, 111, 116–17
  of self, 29–31
Vroom, V.H., 68

Winer, B.J., 68
women managers:
  assets of, 28–29, 38, 40–41, 203–4
  handicaps of, 7, 12–14, 28–29, 32–36, 70
  special problems of, 168–70, 219–23
work, organization of. *See* Time-planning